The Ultimate Anger Management Self-Help Guide

How To Take Complete Control Over Your Emotions, Make Your Relationships Thrive, And Tame The Lion Inside Of You For Good.

Ryan Clark

Table of Contents

Introduction

Sometimes, your anger gets the better of you and takes complete control over you. It stops you from thinking and reasoning clearly. You scream and shout at people, and in some instances, your throw and break things or even get into physical confrontations. Your anger might already have cost you something very important, such as a friend, a job, or even your marriage. Maybe you have even spent a night in jail because of something you did in a fit of rage.

If you identify with any of the above situations, you already know that you have an issue with your anger and that you need to do something about it. You might even have tried doing something about it but to no avail. Most of the advice by experts out there just does not seem to work. You might even have come close to giving up on your anger problem.

Fortunately, this book is here to change all that. After struggling with an anger problem myself, I set out on a mission to learn everything I could about anger and how to deal with it. This book is the result of that mission. I share the same secrets that helped me get over my anger problem and reclaim relationships that had gone awry because of my problem. Inside, you will learn everything about anger, including what exactly it is, why you experience anger, why it is not good for you and how you can control it. I also teach you ancient secrets from Buddhist monks that will give you complete mastery over your emotions and help you to gain total control over your anger. By the time you are done with this book, you will be ready to exercise complete control over your anger and regain complete control of your life.

Ready to start reclaiming your life? Let's meet inside!

Chapter One: What Is Anger?

You are extremely tired after a long day at work and cannot wait to get home and get some rest. On the way home, someone cuts you off in traffic and triggers off your irritation. You start fuming and hurl expletives at him. When you get home, your son says that he has a school project the next day and wants you to get some stuff from the store for him. So much for a relaxing night. After the trip to the store, you come back and immediately fall asleep, only to be woken by the alarm after what feels like two hours. It is morning, but you feel like you haven't slept. You wake up irritated and start shouting orders at everyone. On your way to work, someone rear ends your car and you feel like you are ready to explode. Your heart starts racing, your breathing becomes fast and your body temperature rises. You almost pick a fight, and it takes a lot of calming by your wife to let things go. Even if you avoid getting into a physical confrontation, you are sure of one thing – you are angry!

We have experienced situations that triggered us and made us so angry to the extent we ended up yelling at others or in some cases, resorted to violence. But do you know what exactly anger is or why it makes you feel that way?

Anger is as a natural emotion that is characterized by antagonism towards a person, a thing or a situation that you feel has wronged you in one way or another. Anger is a fundamental emotion, which means that everyone experiences it from time to time, although sometimes the anger is unwanted or irrational. People express anger in varying degrees, from mild forms such as dislike, irritation and displeasure to more extreme forms such as frustration, rage and disgust.

Anger is a secondary emotion, which means that it often stems from another deeper emotion (the primary emotion), such as fear or sadness. Primary emotions are the emotions we feel first after an experience, while secondary emotions are emotions arising from the secondary emotions. To make this easier to understand, let's consider a situation where a man is angry at his spouse because he caught her cheating. In this situation, the man's anger stems from the sadness and disappointment of being betrayed by his spouse.

Primary feelings such as sadness and fear usually cause discomfort to most people. They make you feel helpless, vulnerable and without control over your situation. To avoid this uncomfortable feeling, people resort to anger. Anger often spurs a person to take some action (such as yelling, cursing, breaking things or even fighting), which gives the person a sense of control over the situation. The uncomfortable feeling of a primary emotion cannot cause anger on its own. For one to resort to anger, the primary emotion has to be accompanied by anger-triggering thoughts. Anger-triggering thoughts may occur when a person evaluates a situation and comes to the conclusion that another person is trying to hurt them. Because of this, anger can also be described as a social emotion. This means that anger is always directed at a target (the source of the threat).

Anger is an unpleasant emotion that lets us know when we are unsatisfied with something in our environment. More specifically, anger expresses itself when we think or feel that our physical or emotional well-being is being threatened. Getting injured or being threatened with physical injury, being treated unfairly, getting criticized, facing obstacles that prevent you from achieving your goals are all examples of situations that might make you feel angry because they threaten your physical or emotional well-being. The anger focuses your attention on whatever is threatening your well-being and spurs you to take action to neutralize the threat.

Feelings of anger vary from person to person. Some people get angry at the slightest provocation, while others might tolerate a lot of provocation before they get angry. Some experience very intense anger which might cause them to take very drastic actions, while others only experience mild forms of anger. For some, the feeling of anger will last only a few minutes, while others might continue to feel angry for longer periods of time. Some get angry all the time, while others rarely get angry. The intensity of anger also depends on a person's vulnerability and the magnitude of the perceived threat. If a person's vulnerability is high, even the smallest threat will lead to high-intensity anger. Similarly, when the perceived threat is of a high magnitude, the more intense the anger. Despite all these differences in how different people experience anger, it is a normal emotion that cannot be avoided completely.

Like all emotions, anger affects more than your state of mind. It also has an impact on your body and physiological processes. When you get angry, your blood pressure rises, your heart rate increases, your muscles tense up and your adrenaline levels spike as your body prepares for a confrontation with the perceived threat. Your brain releases chemicals known as catecholamines, which provide you with a burst of energy to help you neutralize the threat. This upsurge in energy is the reason why angry people have a desire for immediate action. Your attention becomes focused on the perceived threat, which explains why it might be difficult for an angry person to think logically. At that moment in time, you are in a primal state where the only thing that matters is to square up with the target of your anger.

Despite being a normal and natural human emotion, anger can become destructive when it gets out of control. Uncontrolled anger impairs a person's thinking and judgment and can lead to rushed, irrational and unreasonable decisions and actions. It can lead to frayed personal and professional relationships, affect one's quality of life, increase one's risk of early death, and cause a ton of other problems, which we will discuss in greater detail in Chapter Four.

Types of Anger

People express different types of anger, depending on their personality, their moods, and the circumstances that caused the anger. Some of the most common types of anger are:

Assertive Anger

This is considered as one of the healthiest ways of expressing anger. A person experiencing assertive anger uses the anger as a motivation to induce positive change. The positive change is attained through assertive communication. People who express their anger assertively are not afraid of confrontation, which means they don't internalize the anger, hold grudges or act passive-aggressively towards the target of their anger. At the same time, they do not resort to aggression and uncontrolled outbursts either. Instead, they communicate in a proper fashion, letting the other person know the reason behind their anger. Proper communication also ensures that there is no room for misunderstandings. Because of this, assertive anger does not lead to damaged relationships.

Chronic Anger

People who experience chronic anger are habitually angry. These people are often angry with almost everything, including themselves. It is like they are constantly looking for something to be angry at. People suffering from chronic anger are usually prone to self-harm. Chronically angry people often have a hard time maintaining healthy relationships. Due to its ongoing nature, this type of anger often has a negative impact on a person's health and well-being.

Behavioral Anger

People who experience behavioral anger have less control over their anger. These people tend to become so overwhelmed by their anger that they end up reacting in a physical and often aggressive manner. Someone experiencing behavioral anger will often end up in a physical fight with the target of their anger. If the target of their anger is someone or something they cannot get at, they will resort to other destructive actions, such as breaking or damaging things in their immediate environment. Owing to its aggressive nature, behavioral anger often has negative consequences. For instance, the relationship between a person and the target of their anger might get frayed after a fight. The person might also face assault charges after beating up someone in a fit of anger.

Passive-Aggressive Anger

This type of anger is common amongst people who are usually afraid of confrontations. Since they cannot confront the target of their anger head-on, these people resort to indirect ways of expressing their anger. Outwardly, such a person will remain calm, while they are inwardly seething with anger. This type of anger is usually expressed through passive forms of aggression, such as the silent treatment, sarcastic comments, angry gestures, avoiding eye contact, procrastination, poor posture, veiled mockery, sulking, gossip, avoidance, and so on. Since it is not expressed directly, identifying this type of anger can be very difficult. Sometimes, even the person expressing passive-aggressive anger might be unaware of it. If you find yourself feeling riled yet you have not acknowledged the feeling or communicated your annoyance to the source of the annoyance, you might be experiencing passive-aggressive anger.

Judgmental Anger

People experiencing this type of anger adopt a judgmental view over the target of their anger. This type of anger is a form of loathing or resentment. A person with judgmental anger will assume a morally superior stance over the target of anger while holding themselves blameless. Judgmental anger is usually expressed as sharp criticisms and scathing comments towards the perceived source of their anger.

Overwhelmed Anger

This type of anger is experienced when an individual feels that the circumstances or situation they are going through are too great for them to cope with. Unable to deal with whatever is on their table, the person becomes hopeless and frustrated. Think about a person who has too much to do within a single day – get kids to school, finish a project with a tight deadline, pick someone up from the airport, deliver groceries to the parents, and so on. Such a person might get angered by a very simple thing. In this case, they are experiencing anger because they feel that they have too much on their plate at the moment and cannot handle any more pressures.

Retaliatory Anger

Retaliatory anger is the most common type of anger. This type of anger occurs when a person feels that they have been wronged by the target of their anger. A person experiencing retaliatory anger is driven by the need for revenge against the perceived wrong. Retaliatory anger is confrontational. It is expressed directly. Due to its vengeful nature, retaliatory anger often results in trouble for the target of the anger. People will express retaliatory anger by yelling and shouting at the recipient of their anger. In extreme cases, retaliatory anger might even lead to physical confrontations.

Self-Abusive Anger

This type of anger is usually directed toward oneself. Self-abusive anger is usually characterized by feelings of shame about oneself. This type of anger often results from situations where a person views themselves as weak, incompetent or unworthy. For instance, if a person fails in an interview or fails to take advantage of an opportunity, they might feel incompetent for failing the interview or unworthy for not taking the opportunity, leading to feelings of anger against themselves. Self-abusive anger is usually expressed through behaviors and actions that are meant to harm oneself, such as self-sabotage, eating disorders, substance abuse, negative self-talk, and so on. In some cases, a person experiencing self-abusive anger might also be critical of people around them in a bid to hide their own feelings of low self-worth.

Verbal Anger

This is a type of anger that is expressed verbally. A person might express verbal anger through verbal threats, criticism and ridicule against the other person, intense blaming, insults, and so on. While it is less dangerous than more physical types of anger, verbal anger is a form of emotional abuse against the recipient of the anger.

Volatile Anger

This type of anger is very unpredictable and is one of the most dangerous types of anger. It comes without a warning and is usually very intense and explosive. People with volatile anger get upset very quickly. Their anger is characterized by strong verbal or physical outbursts. Volatile anger goes as quickly as it comes. A person with volatile anger might be raging mad in one instant, and then totally calm in the next instant. This type of anger is often damaging to relationships. People around a person with this type of anger might feel like they always have to be very careful around the person to avoid triggering his anger, and may even opt to avoid such a person altogether.

The above are some of the most common types of anger. It is good to keep in mind that these are not the only types of anger. Anger is an emotion that is as unique as people's personalities, and the above types are simply attempts at categorizing the different types of anger. It's also good to note that some forms of anger might fall in two or more of these types. For instance, if a person resorts to insults against someone they feel has wronged them, this anger can be classified as verbal due to the way it is expressed, and at the same time be classified as retaliatory due to its vengeful intentions.

Is Anger A Bad Thing?

Growing up, we are taught that anger is a negative emotion and that we should learn to suppress and control our anger. But is this true? Is anger necessarily a bad emotion? It is such a bad thing, why then do we all experience this emotion?

The truth is, anger is not necessarily bad. Anger developed as an emotion whose main purpose is to trigger our self-defense and self-preservation instincts. Without the ability to get angry, we would be incapable of taking a stand against unfair or unjust situations. Anger lets us know that something is wrong and that we need to take action to correct the situation. Below are some of the ways in which anger can be beneficial.

It Acts As A Motivating Force

The fundamental purpose of anger is to spur us to take action. You can turn your anger into a positive force by channeling it toward positive endeavors. Normally, when you are angry, you are greatly determined. You want revenge as quickly as possible. Instead of directing your anger towards the perceived threat, you can direct your anger towards a task and let it drive you towards the completion of the task. Channel your anger to the report you are working on, to your workout, or anything else you want to do. The burst of energy that accompanies feelings of anger will keep you going and make you more productive. You can also change anger into a positive force by using it to motivate you toward success. Instead of revenging physically against your perceived aggressor, you can get revenge by achieving great success, using your anger as the force that motivates you to achieve this success. Improvements in civil rights have historically been made as a result of positively channeling anger.

Anger Can Be Good For Relationships

Anger allows you to take a stand against perceived wrongs. This can be a good thing in relationships, provided the anger is expressed in a healthy manner. Imagine a relationship between two people who have been taught that anger is a bad thing and that they should totally repress it. In such a situation, these people will hide their feelings even when the other person does something wrong. With no way to know that what they are doing is wrong, they keep doing it. This ends up hurting the relationship in the long run. On the other hand, people who have no problem expressing their anger assertively will have no problem letting the other person know when they have done something wrong. This way, the other person can stop the wrongdoing, and any problems in the relationship will be addressed and resolved. This leads to better and stronger relationships.

Anger Provides Insights About The Self

Anger can also help us learn more about ourselves. By learning when and why we tend to get angry, we can get insights about inner self and our faults and then use these insights to improve our lives.

Improves Communication

Sometimes, you might notice that what someone is doing is wrong, yet find it challenging to let them know that what they are doing is wrong because you are afraid of offending them. You end up skirting around the issue, which doesn't help anyone. However, if you are angry at whatever they are doing, you don't really care about not offending them. An angry person tells it as it is, which is by far much better than beating around the bush.

Helps You Determine Your Boundaries

Anger can also help you discover what your boundaries are. Do you always feel ticked off when someone does a particular action? For instance, do you feel upset your spouse takes your car without telling you, thereby inconveniencing you? This is a sign that you need to create a boundary around the use of your car.

From the above reasons, it is clear that anger is not necessarily a bad emotion. When expressed and channeled properly, anger can actually be a beneficial emotion. However, the problem arises when we lose control over our anger. When we let anger control us, it turns into a murky emotion that can lead to very negative consequences. Anger is termed as problematic when it becomes a frequent occurrence and occurs at high intensity, resulting in problematic behaviors and consequences such as aggression, health problems, self-harm, damaged relationships, excessive risk-taking and psychological distress.

Chapter Summary

- Anger is a natural emotion characterized by antagonism towards anything that threatens our well-being.

- Anger is a secondary emotion. Anger is usually expressed to mask an underlying primary emotion, such as sadness or fear.

- Anger spurs us to take action to eliminate or neutralize the perceived threat.

- Feelings of anger vary from person to person.

- There are different types of anger, including assertive anger, chronic anger, behavioral anger, passive-aggressive anger, overwhelmed anger, judgmental anger, retaliatory anger, self-abusive anger, verbal anger and volatile anger.

- Anger is not necessarily a bad emotion. It can acts as a motivating force, lead to better relationships, provide insights about oneself, improve communication and help you determine your personal boundaries.

- Despite being a normal and natural human emotion, anger can become destructive when it gets out of control.

In the next chapter, you are going to learn where anger comes from.

Chapter Two: Where Does Anger Come From?

Have you ever wondered where anger comes from? Sometimes, the cause of anger is quite obvious. If a person walks up to you and slaps you, causing you to respond violently, the source of your anger in this instance is very clear. The person threatened your physical well-being, and you expressed anger against this threat against your physical well-being. Sometimes, however, the source of your anger is not so obvious. Have you ever had your kid rush to welcome you home after a long day, and you snapped at the kid without realizing it. In this instance, it might be difficult pinpointing the source of your anger. Your kid did not do anything to threaten your well-being, yet you responded to her angrily.

The truth is that the causes of anger are often complex and multi-faceted. To make it easier to understand where anger comes from, we will look at it from two points of view. First, we will look at the reasons why we get angry, and then look at the factors that influence how we feel and express anger.

Why Do People Get Angry?

In Chapter One, we mentioned that anger is a secondary emotion, meaning that anger is usually a result of a deeper, underlying primary emotion. But what are these primary emotions that lead to anger? Anger is specifically caused by three primary emotions – fear, frustration and pain.

Fear

When something threatens our well-being, we are conditioned to feel fear. Fear is a primal feeling, one that was designed to help us identify and react to danger and threats. When we experience fear, it often triggers anger in order to help us take action to neutralize the perceived threat. In most cases, anger results not from fear for our lives, but from social fears. Anything that threatens our social standing is often met with anger. Faced with things like the possibility of failure or embarrassment, people will often convert these social fears into anger to help them overcome the fears.

People also tend to get angry when their self-identity is threatened. No one wants to be seen as weak, dumb, inferior, bad, or wrong. When other people's actions, beliefs, and opinions threaten our self-image, we often resort to anger as a way to counter this perceived threat and maintain our self-image. Sometimes, the perceived threats do not even have to be real to trigger our fears. For instance, how many times have you seen a guy get in a fight with another guy because he feels the other guy looked at him funny, when in fact the other guy wasn't even aware that he was looking at him? In this case, the first guy feels threatened in some way and resorts to anger to fight this perceived threat, even when there was no threat in the first place.

Frustration

The second primary feeling that results in anger is the feeling of frustration. There is even a common saying that "frustration begets anger and anger begets frustration". We feel frustrated when our goals, desires and expectations are not met, as well as when we feel like we are not in control of whatever situation we find ourselves in. Frustration arises from our inability to change a situation we don't like. Why do we get angry when the internet takes a long time to load a page? Why do we get angry when a coworker leaves all the work to us at work? Why do we get angry when someone fails to do what they had promised to do? In all these situations, our anger is a direct result of our frustrations. You expect your internet to load quickly, your coworker to pull their weight and whoever made a promise to keep it. When these expectations are not met, frustration creeps in and quickly gives way to anger.

Sometimes, frustrations may build up over a long time. These frustrations then compound together and turn into intense anger even at the slightest provocation. For example, someone who has had a long and frustrating day at work will be more likely to curse at someone who cuts in in traffic, compared to someone who is coming from a relaxing vacation.

When you experience anger due to frustration, the anger is directed at whatever object is perceived to be behind the frustration. For instance, if you are trying to finish a presentation on your computer but then it freezes, you might be tempted to hit it. If the object of your frustration is too powerful or directly inaccessible, the aggressive behavior is deflected to a less threatening or more accessible object. This explains why a soccer fanatic might hit his TV when his team concedes a goal.

Pain

Pain and anger usually go hand in hand. As human beings, we are instinctively driven by the pleasure principle. We seek situations that bring us pleasure and avoid situations that bring us pain. Pain is greatly unwanted, and if we find someone is deliberately causing us pain, we convert the pain to anger so that we can take action to stop the pain from continuing. For example, when someone is mean to us, when someone treats us unfairly or when someone we trusted betrays us, this leads to pain, which quickly turns to anger.

Apart from helping a person confront the source of their pain, anger also makes it easier for a person to deal with their pain by acting as a source of distraction. When a person is feeling pain, they generally think about the pain, which in turn intensifies the pain. On the other hand, an angry person is more focused on getting back at those who caused the pain. Instead of thinking of their pain, they are more focused on the other person. In this sense, it is better to be angry than to be in pain. This shift from pain to anger can happen consciously or unconsciously.

Factors That Influence Your Anger

We have seen that anger is usually a result of the primary feelings of either fear, frustration or pain. However, when faced with these primary emotions, different people will feel and express varying amounts of anger. Put in similar situations, people will react differently. For example, when a coworker plays a prank at the office, one person might be amused by the situation, while another person might become really upset. What is the reason behind this? What determines whether a person will get angry or not? Our likelihood of getting angry is influenced by a number of factors, which include:

Personality

Your personality influences how you react to anger-inducing situations. People with some types of personalities are more likely to respond to situations with anger. For instance, competitive and narcissistic personalities are more likely to experience anger. Let's consider a situation where someone cuts in traffic. If the driver who was cut off is a narcissist, he may presume himself to be the most important person on the road and is therefore more likely to get mad at the driver who cut him off. Similarly, if the driver who was cut off is a competitive person, he or she might think of driving as a competition, and is therefore more likely to get angry with anyone who cuts him or her off.

Current Circumstances

A person's circumstances at the time they experience the anger-inducing situation also have an impact on their likelihood of getting angry. If a person is dealing with a number of things in their life at the moment, they are more likely to get angry, even over minor issues. If a person is feeling anxious, nervous or tired, they are also more likely to react angrily to situations. In these situations, a person's vulnerability is heightened, which makes them more predisposed to react strongly to any perceived threat. People are also more likely to respond with anger when they are grieving.

Assessment Of The Situation

A person's tendency to get angry will also be influenced by their assessment and interpretation of anger-inducing situations. For instance, when a person finds a situation to be unjustified, blameworthy, and punishable, they are more likely to resort to anger. A person's interpretation of and reaction to a situation depends on several factors in the person's life, such as:

Childhood and upbringing: People's tolerance towards expressing anger is influenced to a large extent by their upbringing. People who were brought up knowing that it's okay to react aggressively to situations are more likely to express anger in response to situations, while those who were taught that anger is a bad emotion that should be suppressed are less likely to show their anger. Similarly, children who grew up in families where one of the parents had unmanageable anger might tend to think of anger as a terrifying and destructive force and are therefore more likely to suppress their anger.

Past experiences: People who have experienced difficult situations that made them angry without offering a healthy avenue to vent their anger (such as people who have gone through bullying, trauma or abuse) may be harboring feelings of anger deep inside and are more likely to react aggressively to the slightest provocation. In this case, their anger is tied not only to the current situation but also to their past experiences.

Chapter Summary

- Anger usually stems from one or more of these three primary emotions – fear, frustration and pain.

- People turn to anger to help them take action against anything that threatens their social standing.

- Frustration leads to anger because we feel that we have no control over the situation we find ourselves in.

- When faced with pain, a person will consciously or unconsciously convert it to anger to help them stop the pain from continuing.

- Anger also acts as a source of distraction against pain. Instead of focusing on their pain, an angry person focuses on and is more concerned with getting back at the source of their pain.

- A person's likelihood to react angrily to situations is influenced by their personality, their current circumstances and their assessment of the situation. Their assessment of the situation will also be influenced by factors such as childhood and upbringing as well as their past experiences.

In the next chapter, you are going to learn about the signs and symptoms of anger.

Chapter Three: Signs And Symptoms Of An Anger Problem

Anger is a natural emotion, so there is nothing wrong with feeling angry. Life does not always go as we wish, and when this happens, we might end up getting angry. However, while almost everyone experiences anger, sometimes your anger might end up becoming a problem. When your anger frequently gets out of control and affects you or those around you, this is a sign that your anger has become problematic. Unfortunately, most people with anger problems do not even know that they have an anger problem in the first place, which in turn makes it much more challenging to deal with the anger problem. In this chapter, we are going to take a look at some of the signs that may indicate that you have an anger problem.

You Have A Very Short Fuse

People with an anger management problem usually have very little control over their tempers. They have a problem keeping a lid on their anger and will usually explode when they find themselves in any anger-inducing situation. Do you always yell and scream whenever someone does anything to make you angry? Do you feel that getting aggressive is the best way to express your anger? If you have trouble controlling your temper, this is another sign that you have an anger problem. If not addressed, uncontrolled tempers can have very bad consequences.

You Are Angry for No Reason

Do you experience feeling angry but you cannot point to the exact reason behind your anger? We are naturally conditioned to feel angry as a response to threatening or frustrating situations. Feeling angry without no discernible cause is unhealthy and may be an indicator of an anger problem.

You Are Always Blaming Others

Anger is often an accusatory emotion. When we are angry, we tend to feel that someone else is the problem. However, sometimes, *we* are the problem, and in such cases, it is a mature thing to own up to our mistakes and take responsibility for our actions. If you find yourself struggling to own up to your actions and always look for someone to blame when things go wrong, this could be a pointer to an underlying anger problem.

You Cannot Take Criticism

Criticism is a natural part of life. Nobody is perfect, and it is inevitable that someone will criticize you when you do something wrong or when you do not do what is expected of you. Though criticism sounds negative, it may actually help you to correct your shortcomings and improve yourself. Unfortunately, some of us do not take criticism well. If you find yourself losing your temper, getting defensive and attacking the other person when something negative is said about you, this is a sign that you have an anger management problem.

You Get Enraged Over Past Events

When something bad happens to you, it is perfectly normal to feel enraged in the heat of the moment. After some time, however, these feelings of rage subside. You might still feel angry when you think about the incident in future, but your anger will only be mild. However, if you find yourself feeling intensely angry and enraged when you think about an incident that happened in the past, it shows that you have a problem letting go of your anger, and may be a sign that you have underlying anger management issues.

You Get Mad Over Little Things

Life is full of irritants. Your kid leaving his bed unmade. Someone squeezing the toothpaste tube from the middle. The jerk that cuts you off in traffic. The colleague who spills their coffee on your desk. The guy that takes the parking spot you have been waiting for. The friend who runs late when you have plans. Such irritants are unavoidable, and in as much as they irritate us, they are very minor issues, and there is no point in getting worked up over them. If you find yourself getting mad over such minor issues, this may be an indicator that you have an anger problem.

Very Little Patience

We have no control over the world, and there are many times that things do not go according to our expectations. Patience calls for us to accept and tolerate things that go against our expectations without flying off the handle. Some people, however, have very little patience. They will lose their temper anytime something does not go their way. This lack of patience may be a pointer that you have an anger problem.

Disproportionate Anger

Do you find yourself reacting to situations in ways that other people would find excessive? This is a sure fire sign that you have an anger management problem. While different people experience and express anger differently, normal reactions to anger-inducing situations are generally proportional to the seriousness of the circumstances behind the anger. For instance, if you discover that your partner has been unfaithful, it is normal for you to feel enraged. However, if you show the same kind of rage when you discover that your child forgot to make her bed in the morning, the anger response is not proportional to the circumstance, and this is an indicator that you have an anger management problem.

People Are Cautions Around You

How do your friends and relatives behave around you? Are they overly cautious? Do they seem like they are walking on eggshells, trying as hard as they can not to provoke you? Do they try to avoid you? Are your children afraid of you? Do people display defensive body language when they are around you, such as avoiding eye contact and crossing their arms over their chest when talking to you? Do people apologize excessively when they feel that they have wronged you? All these could be indicators that you have anger management problems. People close to you know you well, and if you find them doing any of the above, they probably know that you tend to explode at the slightest provocation and will try to avoid getting you worked up.

You Hold Grudges

Grudges are persistent feelings of resentment towards somebody because you feel that they did something wrong against you. People who hold grudges have a hard time letting go of their anger. It does not matter how long ago an incident happened, they hold on to their anger and let it turn into resentment. They have a hard time forgiving. Grudges are very damaging to relationships. People who hold grudges will keep bringing up the perceived offense and attacking the other person for it, or they might act passively aggressively towards the other person. If you habitually keep grudges when you are wronged, this is a sign of an anger problem because you have trouble releasing your anger.

You Are Overly-Aggressive

How do you react to anger? Do you feel like attacking and hurting others? Do you take out your anger on things around you? If you tend to slam doors, overturn furniture, kick objects near you, break or damage things near you, physically last out at animals and other violent actions, this is a surefire sign that your anger is problematic. If left unchecked, these aggressive displays against objects and animals can quickly turn into violence against other people, resulting in grave consequences both for you and for the other person.

Your Anger Negatively Affects Your Body

We saw in chapter one that anger is more than a state of mind. It triggers physiological responses in your body. Sometimes, however, the effects of anger on your body go beyond the ordinary responses that prepare you for a confrontation. Anger can also cause negative effects like headaches and other bodily distress. If you notice that you tend to experience some kind of bodily distress when you are angry or after a fit of anger, this is a sign that you have a problem.

You Are Cynical of Others

Your attitude towards others can also be a pointer to an anger problem. People with anger problems are highly cynical. They show great contempt for the actions of others while holding themselves and their actions in high regard. They believe that they would never do the things that others do to make them angry, and believe that others are inferior to them because of this. For instance, if a colleague comes across some challenge while working on a project and asks for help, an angry person might think that the colleague is dumb for not being able to figure it out. In reality, no one knows everything, and even the angry person has perhaps been in a situation where they required another person to bail them out. If you notice that you are habitually cynical and disregarding towards others, this could be a sign of an anger problem.

You Are Always Trying To Win The Argument

People with anger problems forget logic once their anger kicks in. They don't back down from a confrontation, and once they get in an argument, they want to make sure that they have the last word. It doesn't matter if their argument is wrong. They are not concerned with addressing the reason behind the argument or resolving the issue. All they care about is coming out as the winner in the argument. Try to think about your attitude during arguments. Do you care more about finding a solution or winning the argument? If it is the latter, then there is a possibility you might have an anger problem.

It Takes Long To Calm Down From Anger

Getting angry is normal, and almost everyone experiences feelings of anger. However, these feelings are short-lived in most people. The majority of people will have calmed down and relaxed in about 30 minutes after experiencing a bout of anger. For some people, however, their anger is a lot more prolonged. Some people will continue feeling angry even several hours after the incident that led to the anger. If this sounds like you, this is a sign that your anger is problematic and needs to be addressed. If left unaddressed, such prolonged feelings of anger can have an adverse effect on your health and others around you.

Your Anger Concerns You

Does something about your anger and how you express it make you feel uneasy? Do you get angry over the fact that you get angry easily? Do you feel worried by the fact that you cannot predict your reactions when someone does something annoying? Do you often find yourself feeling depressed because of something you did while angry? Do you have regrets about it? The fact that you feel that something is wrong with your anger and how you express it is a sign that you have anger issues. Fortunately, this also shows that you are aware of your problem, which makes it easier for you to work on it.

Others Say You Have An Anger Problem

Most times, other people will notice signs of an anger problem in you before you do. Before your anger problem starts affecting you, it will usually start by affecting people that are close to you. Your family, your friends, your colleagues, and so on. If someone close to you says that you might have an anger problem, this is an indicator that something about your anger is off. If several people say this, this is a clear sign that you might actually have an anger problem. People will not just step out of nowhere to claim that you have an anger problem. If several people are saying it, they must have seen something in your behavior to support their claim. You should listen to them and start assessing your behavior to find out if there are actually situations where you have let your anger get the best of you.

The above are some of the signs that you have an anger problem, though they are not the only indicators of an anger problem. If you can relate to five or more of these signs, it might be time for you to start doing something about your anger.

Chapter Summary

- While anger is a natural and healthy emotion, there are some signs that might point out that your anger is problematic.

- People with anger management problems are usually short-tempered.

- If you find yourself feeling angry for no reason, this could be an indicator of an anger problem.

- People with an anger problem are always blaming others, even when they are on the wrong side.

- People with anger problems find it hard to take criticism.

- If you still feel enraged when you think about past incidents, it shows you have trouble letting go of your anger.

- Getting mad over little things and having little patience is a sign of an anger problem.

- People with anger problems usually react in ways that are disproportionate with the cause of their anger.

- If you notice that people are cautious and fearful around you, they might have realized that you tend to explode at the slightest provocation.

- Holding grudges shows that you have trouble letting of your anger.

- Behaving aggressively and damaging things is a clear sign of an anger problem.

- Angry people are typically cynical of others.

- People with anger problems are more concerned with winning the argument than solving the problem.

- If takes a while for you to calm down after a bout of anger, this could be an indicator of an anger problem.

- If something about your anger makes you uneasy, it is a clear indicator that you have anger issues.

- If others say that you have an anger problem, they are probably right.

In the next chapter, you are going to learn why uncontrolled anger is not good for you.

Chapter Four: Why Anger Is Not Good For You

As previously explained, there is nothing wrong with anger itself. In fact, when it is dealt with quickly, expressed in a healthy way and channeled to proper things, anger can sometimes be a good thing. Think about the fight against racism. If some people did not feel angry that people of color were being treated like lesser humans and then channel their anger to fighting for equal rights, people of color would still be working as slaves. In this case, anger was used as a force for positive change.

Unfortunately, anger is not always expressed in the right way. Sometimes, people turn their anger inwards and hold it for extended periods of time. Other times, people are unable to control their anger. They explode and express it aggressively. When anger becomes uncontrollable, it can have grave consequences, both for the angry person and for those around the person. Often, people don't think about the consequences of uncontrolled anger until it becomes too late. Part of being able to manage your anger depends on the ability to make a rational consideration of the possible outcomes of your anger and then making informed decisions based on your considerations. In this chapter, we are going to take a look at some of the downsides of uncontrolled anger and make it clear to you why you need to get a hold on your anger before it becomes too late. Uncontrolled anger affects us in different ways, including:

Health

Your health is one of the things that are greatly affected by uncontrolled anger. High levels of anger over a prolonged period of time result in several negative impacts on your health and physical well-being. First, anger weakens your immune system and increases your overall risk of contracting different diseases. A study conducted at the Harvard University found that by simply thinking about a past incident when you were angry, the levels of antibody immunoglobulin A in your body decrease for up to six hours. These antibodies are the body's first line of defense against illnesses and infections. Therefore, if you are chronically angry, you can bet that your immune system is greatly compromised.

Secondly, anger also increases your risk of experiencing cardiac problems. According to Doctor Chris Aiken, the director of the Mood Treatment Center and a clinical psychiatry instructor in the School of Medicine at the Wake Forest University, your chances of suffering from a heart attack are twice as high during an outburst of anger and in the two hours that follow the outburst. Similarly, the risk of heart disease is increased in people with repressed anger – people who try to suppress their anger or those who express their anger indirectly. Learning to express your anger in a healthy way is important if you want to protect your heart.

Anger also increases your risk of suffering from stroke. A study conducted by a group of researchers from various universities in the United States found that during and in the two hours following an outburst of anger, the risk of suffering a stroke due to bleeding in the brain or a blood clot inside the brain increases by up to three times. They also found out that if you have an aneurysm in one the arteries in the brain, exploding and lashing out in anger increases the risk of rupturing the aneurysm by up to six times.

In addition to a weak immune system and increased risk of stroke and cardiovascular illnesses, high levels of anger also lead to several other health risks, such as hypertension, depression, chest pains, high blood pressure, headaches and migraines, and so on. Another study conducted by Fristad A. from the University of Michigan also found that people who try to suppress their anger have a decreased lifespan compared to those who express their anger in a healthy way. Therefore, it might be a good idea for you to gain control over your anger if you want to avoid these health risks and enjoy a longer life.

Personal Relationships

This is another sphere of life that is greatly affected by your anger problems. Anger problems can really wreak havoc on the relationships you have with your family, your spouse, your children and your friends. First, anger creates fear and distrust in a relationship. If you normally respond to problems by lashing out, the other person in the relationship may start fearing you. For instance, if your spouse notices that you always get angry whenever there is a problem, they might resort to keeping away problems from you. This creates an environment where many problems go unresolved, which can have dire consequences for the relationship.

The effect of fear is especially pronounced when the relationship is not equal. For instance, if you always shout at your children, they will fear you and may even start avoiding you. In this instance, anger becomes responsible for alienating you from your own children. In addition, the children may pick up the behavior from you and end up with anger problems in future. Anger is a learned behavior that your children can learn by observing you.

If you are the type of person who chooses to suppress your feelings of anger instead of communicating them, this can build distance and resentment in your relationship, which is equally damaging. Here is the problem with suppressing your anger. When you bottle up your anger, the feelings of anger do not go away. They continue simmering inside. Any time the other person does something you do not approve of, it gets compounded with the anger that is already simmering inside. At the same time, since you have not expressed your anger, the other person is not aware that something they are doing is upsetting you, so it is likely they might continue doing it and upset you further, thereby increasing the anger you are feeling inside. In due time, this can drive a wedge between the two of you and end up destroying the relationship.

Suppressed anger also creates tension and frustration. Suppressed anger usually finds its way out through passive aggressiveness. When the other person does something, the anger inside you causes you to make wrong conclusions about them and lay blame on them even when they are not at fault. Without knowing why you are doing this, the other person becomes frustrated with the tension that is in relationship since they don't understand where it is coming from. The relationship becomes miserable and the other person might be eventually forced to break it off.

Impaired Judgment

Another major problem with anger is that it affects your cognitive abilities and impairs your judgment. Anger is triggered by the amygdala, an important part of your limbic system. The limbic system is responsible for regulating emotions that are essential for our survival, such as hunger, fear, and anger. Since these emotions are necessary for survival, the limbic system, and the amygdala in particular does not pause to think and consider the long-term consequences of its actions. It is reflexive and automatic. It simply mobilizes the body for immediate action in response to a particular stimulus.

When you are angry, your amygdala is active, while the activity in the cognitive part of your brain, which is more reflective, rational, and slower, is reduced. Therefore, when you are angry, you are more dependent on the amygdala and less on the cognitive part of your brain. Since the amygdala is responsible for triggering impulsive action, you are less likely to consider the outcomes of your actions when you are angry. Any possible consequences that may cross your mind are made to appear insignificant since the amygdala wants you to act immediately, not to waste time thinking. Because of this, you are more likely to engage in irrational actions when you are angry; actions you would not take under normal circumstances. Unfortunately, some of these actions can have very negative consequences, and you might end up regretting them later.

Anxiety And Depression

High levels of anger can also lead to anxiety and depression. According to research conducted by researchers from Concordia University, anger can lead to an increase in the symptoms of generalized anxiety disorder. This is a condition where individuals are so worried about everyday things that it affects their ability to function normally. Anxiety can, in turn, lead to other health problems. To make matters worse, anxiety can also fuel your anger problem. This can lead to a vicious cycle where your anger leads to anxiety, which then makes your anger problem, and the increased anger problem leads to even greater anxiety, and so on. Putting a stop to this cycle can be quite challenging.

Numerous studies have also shown that there is a strong link between anger and depression. In fact, Sigmund Freud used to describe depression as anger that was channeled inwards. For people already suffering from depression, an anger problem exacerbates the symptoms of depression. This is especially common in people who have trouble expressing their anger. These people ruminate on their anger but never take action, which creates a victim mentality and makes their depression even worse.

Work

Uncontrolled anger can also have negative impacts on your work. Anger clouds your judgment and impacts your ability to think clearly and focus. It is difficult to concentrate on the spreadsheet on your computer when all you are thinking about is how your boss humiliated you and how you can get back at him. This can lead to decreased productivity and performance at work. Once you earn a reputation as a person who has a short temper, your relationships and interactions with colleagues may become strained. Colleagues may avoid talking to you or working with you. Colleagues may lose their trust in you and avoid seeking your help even when they are stuck. Customers and clients may start avoiding you or the management might exempt you from taking part in critical and high-priority projects. In extreme cases, your anger can lead to irrational actions such as shouting at your bosses or reacting violently towards a boss or colleague. This can lead to loss of your job, and in some cases, might even lead to a lawsuit.

Safety: Road Rage

Driving is one activity that seems to stress everyone out. Before I learnt how to control my anger, I was so prone to road rage. Another driver would do something I considered stupid and I would get all worked up and start driving aggressively. I was not alone in this. According to a survey conducted in 2016 by AAA, almost 80% of drivers have experienced road rage, with a huge number among them taking action meant to get back at the other driver. Unfortunately, driving with rage and taking action meant to get back at drivers who annoy you can be dangerous. I already noted above that anger impairs your judgment. When you are behind the wheel, the effects of impaired judgment are immediate and in most cases fatal. By driving when you are angry, you put yourself, your passengers and other road users at risk. Many accidents can be directly attributed to road rage. In some cases, people even stop their vehicles and get into physical confrontations. There have been numerous cases of people who have been shot in confrontations that resulted from road rage. Is it really worth dying or killing your children in an accident just because some driver cut you off in traffic? The other driver could even be rushing a sick person to hospital or may be in some other emergency, thus making your road rage unjustified.

Self-Esteem

Uncontrolled or unexpressed anger has also been linked to low self-esteem. When someone with anger problems is feeling angry, they act impulsively, guided by their anger. In this moment of rage, they usually end up doing things that they would not do under normal circumstances. Once their rage has subsided, they might feel guilt, remorse, shame and embarrassment for what they did. Such a person might think they are weak because they have no control over their emotions. These feelings of guilt, embarrassment and the sense of inadequacy over their inability to control their emotions can erode the person's self-esteem. In other instances, a person might have a problem expressing their anger. Unable to confront the source of their anger, such a person turns the anger on themselves because of their inability to stand up for themselves, which in turn leads to reduced self-esteem.

By now I hope you can see why uncontrolled or unexpressed anger is not good for you and why you need to take action once you realize that you might have an anger management problem.

Chapter Summary

- Anger can lead to a lot of negative consequences when it is not expressed in a healthy and constructive way.

- Uncontrolled or unexpressed often has negative effects to your health. It might lead to a weakened immune system, increased risk of cardiovascular problems, increased risk of stroke, and several other health risks.

- Anger can also damage your relationships with family, friends, children or your spouse.

- Anger impairs your judgment and may lead to impulsive and irrational actions that you might end up regretting once your anger has subsided.

- Anger can also lead to anxiety and depression or exacerbate the symptoms if you are already suffering from one of these conditions.

- Uncontrolled anger at work can strain your workplace relationships, and might lead to loss of work and lawsuits in extreme cases.

- Anger when driving can lead to road rage, thereby putting you, your passengers and other road users at risk.

- Uncontrolled or unexpressed anger can also lead to low self-esteem issues.

In the next chapter, you are going to learn about some of the common myths and misconceptions that people hold about anger.

Chapter Five: Common Myths About Anger

In this chapter, you will learn about some common myths about anger. Anger is a very strong emotion, and due to its aggressive and destructive nature when uncontrolled, it is one of the most misunderstood emotions. People have developed several myths and misconceptions about it. Unfortunately, these myths and misconceptions pose a problem. They affect people's views and attitudes towards anger, which in turn makes it harder for people dealing with anger to deal with it in a constructive manner. For you to effectively manage your anger, you need to dispel any myths you might hold about anger. Below are some of the most common myths about anger.

Myth 1: Anger Is A Negative Emotion

From a very young age, most of us are taught that anger is a bad emotion. It is painted as this negative and terrifying emotion that makes you sad and miserable and dampens your enthusiasm for life. We are taught that we should avoid it at all costs. However, anger is not really a negative emotion. It is a perfectly natural emotion that is meant to help us put a stop to anything that threatens our well-being. It protects us from harm and motivates us to push for positive change. Think of all the progress that has been made in the world in regards to equality and justice.

Do you think such progress would have been achieved without people getting angry? Not likely. It is anger that spurs activists around the world to fight against social injustices. Anger only becomes a negative emotion when we choose to express it in negative ways.

Myth 2: Anger Is Aggressive And Destructive

This myth is closely related to the previous one. We have been conditioned to think of anger as an aggressive and destructive force that makes things worse instead of helping us solve them. When you think of the word anger, you automatically associate it with shouting and yelling, fights and physical confrontations, breaking things around you and so on. This view of anger stems from the fact that most people with anger problems express their anger in destructive ways. For every person who expresses their anger destructively, there are several people who express their anger in a constructive manner. While anger is a normal and healthy emotion, expressing it through aggression and destruction is not healthy. One can deal with anger without being aggressive and destructive.

As a matter of fact, expressing anger through aggression and destruction is less effective than expressing it through calmness and assertiveness. Consider a situation where you were supposed to attend an event with a friend but he arrives late and you end up missing the event. Since it was important for you to attend the event, you will naturally be feeling upset. You might respond by yelling at your friend, though this will only make him get on the defensive, and it's unlikely that this will get him to improve on his tardiness. On the other hand, if you respond to him assertively without resorting to name-calling, he is more likely to change his behavior. For instance, you might say, *"This was a very important event for me, and I'm upset with you for being so late that we ended up missing the event."* This way, you are not attacking or threatening your friend, you are expressing your anger in a productive manner.

Myth 3: Anger Is A State Of Mind

People wrongly assume that anger exists only in the mind. Therefore, when trying to control their anger, they only concentrate on what's going on in their head. However, there is more to anger than just what is going on in your mind. Anger also manifests itself throughout your body. Think of what happens to your body when you are angry. Your blood pressure rises, your heart rate increases, your hands start shaking, your respiration rate goes up, your face gets flushed, and the hairs on the back of your neck stand up. These physiological responses contribute to your anger and aggressive behavior. Therefore, when trying to control your anger, you should focus on more than your mind – you should also focus on calming your body.

Myth 4: Men Are Generally Angrier Than Women

There is a common view in society, perpetrated by mainstream media and literature, that men and boys are generally more prone to displays of anger than women and girls, and that men's and boys' anger is more justified. In fact, if you perform an image search for 'angry person' on Google, you will notice that a very high percentage of the images are men. But is this view that men are generally angrier true? Well, research conducted by NBC and Esquire shows that women get angry more frequently and at higher rates than men. The notion that men are generally angrier stems from the fact that men are more likely to express their anger impulsively and in an aggressive manner, which makes it more visible. Women tend to use passive-aggressive methods to express their anger.

Myth 5: Ignoring Your Anger Will Make It Go Away

There is a very common misconception that your anger will magically go away if you ignore it. Growing up, many of us are told to suppress our anger for the sake of maintaining peace. This is a very wrong view of anger that does a lot of damage. Many marriages and relationships get broken because of the built-up resentment when people refuse to address their anger.

Imagine you are driving on your way home and then the red warning light on your car comes on. Would you cover it with a piece of tape and assume that the problem has gone away because you can no longer see the light? I think not. Covering the warning light is a superficial solution that does nothing to deal with the actual problem. Ignoring your anger is like covering the warning light on your car with a piece of tape.

Remember, anger is an emotion that is meant to help us notice when something in our environment is wrong. When you ignore your anger, you avoid dealing with the reason behind the anger. This means that the problem persists and will keep making you angry. If you keep ignoring this anger, it will build up and become a bigger problem that you will have to deal with at a later date. Various research and studies also show that ignoring your anger can affect your health adversely, increasing the risk of heart attack and early death. This makes this particular myth quite detrimental. Not only does it keep you from solving the problem that is triggering your anger, it can also send you to an early grave.

Myth 6: Venting Your Anger Will Make You Feel Better

We already noted that people wrongfully believe that anger is an aggressive and destructive force. This misconception is the basis of the myth that one can release their anger and feel better by finding a physically aggressive mechanism for venting their anger. If you look around the internet, many people will advise you to find a physical release for your anger. Throw and break some plates. Go outside and scream your heart out. Punch your pillow. Go to the gym and spend an hour with the punching bag. Punch holes in a wall. Trash your room. There are even companies that have turned 'destruction therapy' into a business opportunity. They provide anger rooms where you can go in and let off your anger by smashing junk with a baseball bat. But does this destruction therapy really work?

Various studies suggest that venting your anger through such aggressive mechanisms does not actually release your anger. Instead, trying to release your anger through aggression, even in a controlled environment, only increases and reinforces aggressive responses to anger. Instead of helping you deal with your anger, venting your anger aggressively makes you better at being angry. Another study by psychologist Brad J. Bushman found that doing nothing in response to your anger is actually more effective than venting your anger aggressively.

Myth 7: Anger Is Hereditary

People often assume that anger is an inherited problem. How many people have you heard claiming that they have anger issues because one of their parents had an anger problem and passed them to him or her? The truth is that anger is a learned behavior. The misconception that anger is hereditary stems from the fact that a person's attitude towards anger is learned by observing influential people in the person's life. Therefore, if your parents had anger problems, often resorting to aggression as a way of dealing with their anger, it is likely you will learn the same behavior from them. This might people think that the behavior was passed from your parents genetically rather than through observation.

The problem with this misconception is that it makes it difficult for people to deal with their anger issues. This myth implies that their anger problems are permanent. After all, if a certain behavior is in your genes, there is nothing you can do to change it. Fortunately, anger is not a genetic condition. It is a learned behavior, which means that you can change the behavior by learning new, appropriate ways of expressing your anger.

Myth 8: Outside Stimuli Make Us Angry

Another common misconception is that it is usually other people, events or things that make us angry. This misconception stems from the fact that anger is a targeted emotion. Whenever you are feeling angry, your anger is directed towards a person or object that you feel is the source of your anger. Think about a situation where you were angry about something. You might say something like, *"He made me so angry, I couldn't help yelling at him"* or *"The rain makes me so mad when I'm driving."*

The truth is that anger is an inside job. People, events and things are not the causes of your anger. They are merely triggers. Your anger stems from your reaction towards the trigger. In other words, being angry is a choice you make yourself. For instance, imagine a situation where you were supposed to meet your friend for lunch. You wait inside the restaurant for a whole hour but your friend does not show up. You get so agitated because all the time she has kept you waiting. You might even decide that you will never go out for lunch with her again. Now imagine the same situation, but after keeping you waiting for an hour, your friend calls and said that she got involved in a minor accident and got held up because she had to deal with the police. Even if you were angry, your anger will dissipate in the second situation. Two similar situations, yet two different reactions.

Similarly, imagine a situation where you left the house with plans to get to town in 30 minutes. Unfortunately, you find that there is a lot of traffic and you end up spending an hour on the road before you get to town. In this situation, you might get very irritated by the traffic. However, if you left the house anticipating that there will be traffic and you'll spend an hour on the road, you are less likely to get mad. Once again, two similar situations yet two different reactions.

These two examples show that anger is a personal choice. The traffic and your friend's lateness are merely triggers. The choice on whether to react angrily or calmly to the trigger lies squarely on you. Claiming that other people, things or events are the source of your anger allows you to shift the blame to an outside factor and avoid taking responsibility for your anger.

Myth 9: Behaviors Stemming From Anger Are Uncontrollable

This is another myth that people use to avoid taking responsibility for anything they do when they are angry. How many times have you heard an angry person say something like, *"When I get angry, I can't control myself!"* or *"I was so enraged, I didn't even realize what I was doing."* Such statements imply that when a person is angry, they have no control over their actions. It would seem that the strong feelings associated with anger automatically lead to specific behaviors that we can do little to prevent.

However, the truth is that we have total control over our behavior even when we are engulfed in a rage. Anger is an emotion like any other. How could it be possible that only this one emotion leads to uncontrollable behaviors in a way no other emotion is capable of? Think of people who tend to show aggressive behaviors when angry. Such a person might get violent towards a spouse when they are alone, yet will be able to control their anger if there is another person around at the time the person's anger was triggered. Similarly, a person might get violent towards a spouse when enraged, yet they would never get violent towards their boss in a similar fit of rage. This shows that behaviors stemming from anger are actually controllable. By making such behaviors appear automatic and uncontrollable, people are looking for a way to avoid holding themselves responsible for their actions.

Myth 10: Anger Has To Be Released Once It Builds Up

People often treat anger like a coiled spring. When a spring is coiled, it contains a lot of potential energy and will explode the moment it is released. People commonly think the same thing about anger. When you get angry, the anger is treated like some sort of potential energy that increases the pressure within your body. It is assumed that the only way to reduce this pressure is to find a way to release it. This view of anger is a misconception. The truth is that anger is more of an idea than a physical energy. Remember the example I used earlier about waiting for a friend you were supposed to have lunch with? After waiting for your friend for an hour, you might be very upset with her. However, when the friend calls and says that she has been involved in an accident, the anger suddenly dissipates. Where did it go? Note that you did not do anything to release your anger. It simply disappeared. In this case, your anger disappears because you changed your perception of the situation that triggered your anger. Initially, you assumed that your friend was keeping you waiting deliberately, which can be translated to a deliberate attempt to hurt you. However, once you learn that she was not doing it deliberately, there is no reason behind your anger, and therefore it goes away. This shows that one can stop being angry without having to do anything to release their anger.

Chapter Summary

- Learning to tell facts about anger from myths will make it easier for you to deal with your anger effectively and constructively.

- Anger is not always a negative emotion. It only becomes negative when expressed in negative ways.

- Anger is not always an aggressive and destructive force. One can deal with anger without being aggressive and destructive.

- Anger is more than a state of mind. It also affects your body. When trying to control your anger, you should focus not only on calming your mind, but also your body.

- Men are not generally angrier than women. Men only seem to be angrier because they express their anger in impulsive and aggressive ways, which are more visible.

- Ignoring your anger will not make it go away. Instead, it keeps you from solving the problem behind the anger and affects your health negatively.

- Venting your anger aggressively does not help you deal with your anger. Matter of fact, it only makes you better at being angry.

- Anger problems are not hereditary. Anger is a learned behavior, which means that you can change it by learning new and constructive ways of expressing your anger.

- Anger is not caused by other people or things outside our control. These merely trigger our anger. Getting angry is a choice you make by yourself.

- Anger does not automatically result in behaviors that we have no control over. You have total control over any action you take when angry.

- Anger is not a physical energy that has to be released for you to feel better. You can control your anger by changing your perception of the situation that triggered the anger.

In the next chapter, you are going to learn how you can stop being easily irritable.

Chapter Six: How To Stop Being Easily Irritable

In this chapter, we are going to take a look at how you can reduce your irritability and prevent minor issues from escalating into full-blown anger. Sometimes, the frequency and intensity of your anger increase not because of the actual events that trigger your anger, but because your irritability is high. When you are feeling irritable, you are already in a state of arousal. Your tolerance to anger triggers is significantly low, which means that you are more likely to get frustrated easily. Things that you would ordinarily ignore get you upset more easily and your response to stressful situations becomes more aggressive. This is not a good thing, especially if you have an anger problem.

Common wisdom dictates that prevention is better than cure. It is far better to prevent your anger than to deal with it once it has been triggered. Luckily, there are some steps that you can take to reduce your irritability and therefore keep your anger at bay. Some of these steps include:

Look At Things From The Other Person's Perspective

This is a great tactic for situations where your irritability is a direct result of something another person has done. Sometimes, we are so focused on our own feelings and emotions that we don't take a moment to think about what other people might be going through. By taking a moment to consider things from the other person's perspective, we can become more tolerant to anger triggers. For instance, if someone cuts you off in traffic, this might naturally make you irritated. However, if someone told you that the person was rushing their sick kid to hospital, you would be more understanding of their behavior. Unfortunately, there is no one to explain to you the reason behind the other person's actions, so it is up to you to try and look at things from their point of view and give them the benefit of doubt. So, next time someone does something you don't approve of, instead of assuming that they are a jerk and getting irritated by their behavior, it is better to assume that they have a problem that might be affecting their behavior.

Learn To Let Things Go

Sometimes, we become irritated because we are obsessed with small to medium size issues that do not have any major impact in the grand scheme of things. For example, maybe your husband squeezes the toothpaste tube from the middle, or maybe he cannot remember to leave the toilet seat down. Instead of getting irritated by something like this and letting it ruin your entire morning, it is better to take a few minutes to remind yourself that this does not have any major impact on your life, unless you want it to. Leaving the toilet seat up does not hurt you in any way. Rather than shouting at your husband about it for the umpteenth time, just let it go and lower the seat yourself. It will only take you two seconds to do that. Instead of constantly thinking of a minor annoying thing someone does, focus on what you like about them and you are less likely to get irritated by these pet peeves.

Adopt Open-Mindedness

In Chapter Two, I mentioned that one of the reasons behind feeling angry is the frustration that results from unfulfilled expectations. When faced with something unexpected, we experience anxiety and fear of the unknown, which in turn increases our irritability. When you set out for work in the morning, you don't expect that there will be massive traffic because of an accident on the highway. When you realize that you will be late, this leads to anxiety and fear. Will the boss notice that you got to work late? This small issue can end up making you irritable throughout the whole day.

To avoid getting irritated by such things, you should adopt an open mind and let go of expectations over things you cannot control. Most times, our expectations are irrational. You expect that traffic will be smooth, yet you cannot control traffic. You cannot stop an accident from happening. Instead of letting these unexpected things get to you, acknowledge that anything might actually happen and there is nothing you can do about it. By adopting such a mindset, you won't be caught by surprise when something unexpected happens. Instead of feeling disoriented by the unexpected, you will focus on how to deal with it. This will make you less anxious and keep your irritability at bay.

Get Some Sleep

Does it seem like everyone is out to get you after a night of poor sleep? The traffic seems extraordinarily slow, you see your kids as a nuisance and your colleagues seem like they made a bet to see who will annoy you the most. Turns out that these reactions are totally normal, according to science. Various studies show that there is a strong link between lack of sleep and increased irritability. Lack of sleep leads to increased activity to the part of your brain known as the amygdala, whose main function is to detect threats and trigger negative emotions such as pain and fear. At the same time, lack of sleep inhibits the connection between the amygdala and the part of the brain responsible for regulating the functions of the amygdala. This means that when you do not get enough sleep, you are more likely to get irritated easily, and at the same time, your ability to deal with irritation is increased.

Therefore, if you want to reduce your irritability, you should make sure that you get enough sleep every night. If possible, ensure that you get 7 to 9 hours of sleep each night. You should also make sure that you are getting good quality sleep. To do this, ensure that your sleeping environment is conducive for sleeping. Keep your bedroom cool, dark and quiet. You should also avoid foods and drinks that interfere with your sleep before bedtime and establish a relaxing pre-sleep routine, such as taking a bath or reading a book. If possible, you should also stick to a regular sleeping schedule. This regulates your internal clock and allows you to fall asleep faster and get better sleep.

Incorporate Some Alone Time In Your Day

Sometimes, you might be feeling more irritable because you have a lot on your mind. Your mind is literally overwhelmed by all the things you are thinking about – the yard that needs to be mowed, your child's upcoming graduation, your stretched finances, the speech you need to give, and so on. All the worrying, planning, considering, analyzing and obsessing uses up your mental resources and leaves you tired. Your brain sees this decrease in mental resources as a vulnerability and therefore increases its sensitivity to perceived threats. This is why you become highly irritable when there is a lot on your mind.

To prevent wearing your mind out with all the things you are thinking about, you should start incorporating some quiet alone time in your day to day schedule. This can be the first hour when you wake up, the last hour before you sleep or even some time during the day. During your chosen alone time, disconnect off from anything that might distract you – the TV, your cell phone, the computer and so on. Instead, find a book to read, take a nature walk, listen to music, or have a relaxing bath. During this time, you should avoid thinking any of the things that need to be done and focus on yourself.

Spending some time alone and in relative calmness allows your brain to rest, unwind and replenish itself. By taking the time to do this, your mental resources will be constantly renewed and you will be in a better position to handle stressors without getting irritated.

Become More Assertive

Sometimes, our irritability is a direct result of annoyances caused by people stepping beyond our boundaries. A colleague might make an inappropriate comment about you and annoy you, leaving you irritated throughout the day. Your partner might take your car on an errand without letting you know, resulting in you being late for an appointment, and because of this, you remain grumpy throughout the day. In both situations, your annoyance is the direct result of someone not respecting your boundaries. However, the person might not even be aware of these boundaries.

To avoid such annoyances, you should learn to set and communicate your boundaries more assertively. Assertiveness means being able to express yourself and your feelings to others effectively and being able to stand up for your rights, without disrespecting the rights of others. Being assertive can help you reduce your irritability in a number of ways. First, by standing up for yourself, you earn the respect of others. People stop mistreating you or taking you for granted, which means less annoyances. Second, assertiveness can also boost your self-esteem. People with a higher self-esteem are generally more tolerant to annoying situations, which means they are less likely to get irritated by minor issues.

Finally, assertive people are better at putting their needs ahead of those of others, which leads to lower stress levels and therefore less irritability. For instance, if a friend calls to vent about a bad day when you are busy at work, you might be inclined to allow them to vent while putting your work on hold. Since you have a tight deadline, your friend's perceived disregard for your time might annoy you, but you still allow them to go on. An assertive person, on the other hand, would sympathize with the friend, tell the friend that they are busy at the moment and ask the friend to call later. By doing so, the assertive person avoids the annoyance that would have resulted from the situation.

Going back to the above examples, if your colleague makes an inappropriate remark about you, make it clear to them that you will not stand such remarks. If your partner takes your car without your permission, let him or her know that this is wrong. If someone wants you to help them with something when you have other things on your table, don't be afraid to say no. By setting clear boundaries and becoming more assertive in enforcing these boundaries, you will reduce the annoyances that stem from day to day interactions with people around you.

Check Your Eating Habits

Ever heard of the saying that a hungry man is an angry man? There is a lot of truth in this statement. Food affects your state of mind. Various studies show that there is a strong link between low blood sugar and negative mood states. Therefore, the next time you experience highly irritable, you should check your eating habits, since low blood sugar might be the cause of your moodiness.

To ensure that your blood sugar levels remain steady throughout the day, you should make it a habit to eat and snack regularly. This ensures that there is a constant supply of fuel in your body and therefore keeps you from becoming grumpy. You should avoid skipping meals, since this will lead to decreased blood sugar levels and result in increased irritability. The kind of food you eat also affects your mood. Avoid foods that are all quick-release sugars. While this will give you an immediate spike in blood sugar levels, the spike will be short-lived, and when the levels go back down your mood is likely to be worse than before you had the sugary food. You should also add more proteins in your meals. Proteins increase the levels of dopamine in your body. Dopamine is the feel-good hormone, and increased levels of dopamine will improve your mood and decrease your irritability.

Get Organized

If you thought that leaving piles of laundry in your bedroom and unwashed dishes on the sink has no effect on how you feel, think again. Mess and clutter affect all aspects of your life, including your moods, and might be the reason you are feeling so cranky. A study conducted at the University of California found that people who spend time in cluttered environments had higher levels of the cortisol, indicating that they were more stressed, fatigued and moody. Next time you find yourself feeling edgy, your environment might be the sole culprit.

If mess and clutter is the reason behind your irritability, you can reduce the irritability and feel calmer by taking a moment to organize your surroundings. Organize your living space, spread your bed, wash the dirty dishes, fold the pile of clothes in your bedroom and make sure your workspace is neat and tidy. This simple thing will improve your mood and make it easier for you to deal with stressing situations without getting angry.

Have Some Fun

Having fun does a number of things that can help you become less irritable and become better at handling stressful situations. First, having fun allows you to let go of any thoughts that might be overwhelming your mind. Think of the last time you had fun. Your mind becomes focused on the moment. No thinking about the pending bills or the projects that need to be completed. Secondly, fun activities act as a buffer against stressing situations. Engaging in pleasurable activities lowers the levels of cortisol in your body while increasing the levels of serotonin. This increases your moods and makes you better equipped to deal with stressors.

While modern life is hectic and filled with busy schedules, you should make some time to let everything go, relax and engage in some pleasurable activities. Go to the movies, go swimming, go out on a date with your partner, go hiking, play a sport you enjoy, or do anything else that allows you to relax and have fun. Doing this frequently will increase your tolerance to events that tend to trigger your anger.

Get More Exercise

When most people think about exercise, they often associate it with increased physical well-being. However, exercise does more than just keeping you fit. It also has an effect on your mental well-being and your moods, and can be the perfect solution for your irritability. Aerobic exercise, in particular, is good at alleviating anger. The positive effects of aerobic exercise on your moods have a neurochemical basis. When you engage in aerobic exercise, the levels of stress hormones in your body, such as cortisol and adrenaline, are reduced. At the same time, exercise triggers the release of dopamine and endorphins, which are the body's natural mood elevators. The release of these two hormones generally makes you happier and increases your tolerance to stressors, which means that you are less likely to feel irritable.

To decrease your irritability in the long-term, you should make exercising a part of your regular routine. If possible, try to get at least 30 minutes of physical activity every day. Exercising does not necessarily mean going to the gym. You can exercise by taking a walk, going for a run, swimming or engaging in a sport you enjoy. It is even better if you can perform these activities outdoors, since being out in nature also has a positive effect on your moods.

Learn To Meditate

Meditation can be a great solution for you if you have the tendency to get irritated over the tiniest things. A study conducted by researchers from the Department of Psychology at the University of Kansas found that a single session of meditation lowers your response to anger-inducing situations. Not only does meditation reduce your emotional response to anger triggers, it also reduces the physical signs of anger. It makes you calmer and increases your ability to cope with negative situations without reacting negatively. Meditation also makes it easier for you to recognize when you are reacting to distressing thoughts and to let go of such thoughts.

If you have the tendency to get irritated easily, you should try and make meditation a part of your daily routine. It doesn't have to take a lot of your time. Meditating for just 20 minutes every day can do wonders for your irritability. Simply find a quiet and comfortable place where you will not be disturbed, sit with your eyes closed and focus on your breathing. Try to let go of all thoughts. You can do this by focusing your mind on the feeling of the air coming in and out of your nose, or on a mental image of a peaceful place, such as a quiet beach with rolling waves. If you find your attention being drawn to a particular thought, that is normal, just let it go. If learning to meditate on your own seems challenging, find guided meditation apps, download them on your phone and use them during your meditation sessions.

Boost Your Self-Esteem

Sometimes, your irritability might also be a direct result of low self-esteem. People with low self-esteem don't think much of themselves. They believe they don't bring anything to the table. These feelings of insignificance can turn into repressed feelings of anger and hurt, and when left to build up, they can manifest themselves as extreme irritability. In addition, people with low self-esteem are overly sensitive. Anything someone else says about them gets to them, making them more prone to respond negatively to even the lightest comment.

If you are highly irritable due to low self-esteem, you can tame your irritability by boosting your self-esteem. There are a number of things you can do to improve your self-image. Focus on your strengths instead of your weaknesses. Don't berate yourself for your mistakes. It is natural to make mistakes. Learn to express yourself and your feelings instead of letting them simmer. If someone says something unfair about you, stand up for yourself and say you disagree with them, instead of letting it get to you and affect your moods. As you self-image starts improving, you will start becoming less irritable.

Uncover The Reason Behind Your Irritability

Sometimes, your irritability might be an indicator of an underlying problem. For instance, if you are going through problems with your significant other that you have not resolved, if you are not happy at work, or if you have some other issue that might be stressing you out, this can lead to increased irritability. Try to introspect and find out if there is an unresolved problem that might be manifesting itself through your irritability. Unless you solve the underlying problem, you will not be able to tame your irritability. If you are having issues in a personal relationship, talk with the other person, get to the root of the problem and try to resolve it. If your work is the source of your stress, it might be time to consider making a career change.

Health issues like hormonal imbalance in women, hyperthyroidism, premenstrual syndrome, diabetes, lung disease, cardiovascular disease, and menopause, as well as psychological problems like anxiety and depression can also lead to increased irritability. If your irritability feels out of control, if you are constantly irritated, if you are experiencing more angry outbursts than usual, or if you feel like your irritability is getting worse, these might be signs of an underlying health or psychological issue. If you notice any of these signs, it might be wise to go to your doctor for a checkup to find out if there is an underlying medical problem.

Chapter Summary

- When your irritability is high, you tend to get angry quicker and more frequently, even over minor things that you would ordinarily ignore.

- It is far better to prevent your anger than to deal with it once it has been triggered.

- Learn to look at things from the other person's perspective before concluding that they are just being a jerk.

- Learn to let go of minor annoyances that have no significant impact instead of letting them ruin your mood.

- Learn to express your anger assertively.

- You can reduce your irritability by being more open-minded and acknowledging that life is full of unexpected things that you have no control over.

- You irritability might be an indication that you are not getting enough rest. You should improve your sleeping habits and ensure that you get proper rest each night.

- Incorporating some alone time in your day to give your mind time to recharge itself will make you less irritable.

- Set and assertively maintain boundaries to avoid getting annoyed by people who try to overstep your boundaries.

- Your eating habits have an effect on your mood. Improving your eating habits can help reduce your irritability.

- Ensuring your immediate environment is organized can help you reduce your mental clutter, which is often the reason behind your irritability.

- Finding time to have fun improves your moods and makes you less irritable.

- Exercising lowers stress hormone levels in your body and triggers release of feel good hormones, leading to better moods and increased tolerance to stressors.

- Meditation makes you calmer, lowers your response to anger-inducing situations and increases your ability to cope with negative situations without reacting negatively.

- Your irritability might also be caused by low self-esteem. Take action to improve your self-image and you will see a significant decrease in your irritability.

- Uncover the underlying reason behind your irritability and take action to solve it. If you cannot pinpoint the reason behind your irritability, it might be wise to talk to your doctor, since irritability can also be an indication of an underlying medical condition.

In the next chapter, you are going to learn how to get to the root of your anger.

Chapter Seven: How To Get To The Root Of Your Anger

In Chapter One, we saw that anger is a secondary emotion, which means that there is usually an underlying emotion behind the anger. Sometimes, the underlying emotion is quite obvious. For instance, when someone intentionally bumps into you when you are walking down the road, you might react with anger. You may feel that it was deliberate. By deliberately bumping into you, the other person is essentially threatening you, and it is easy to tell that your anger is a direct response to this threat. Sometimes, however, the reason behind your anger is not so obvious.

Sometimes, your anger might be rooted in self-esteem issues that you might not even be aware of. The anger might be a way of masking these problems. Other times, your anger might be rooted in painful memories about something that happened to you in the past, perhaps even during your childhood. In this case, your anger could be your brain's way of automatically distracting you from this pain. It gives you a sense of control over your vulnerability and fear. Anger essentially tells us that something is wrong, though it does not necessarily what that is. Unfortunately, anger spurs us to take action, which means that sometimes we might take action without even knowing what the real issue is.

The first step to dealing with anger is to ask yourself an important question: why are you so angry? Only by answering this question and uncovering the actual reason behind your anger will you be able to effectively deal with it. Sometimes, getting to the actual reasons behind your anger might need a lot of time and a lot of digging. However, without uncovering the underlying issues behind your anger, trying to address your anger problem will be like treating the symptoms while doing nothing about the actual illness. In this chapter, we are going to look at some tactics and techniques you can use to dig deeper and find the root cause of your anger.

Recognize That You Are Getting Angry

In order to know to get to the root of your anger problem, you need to learn to recognize when you start getting angry. Many people with an anger problem might not even notice when their anger starts rising. They only notice it once it is already boiling and getting out of control. So, the first thing you need to do is to take notice of your anger once it starts rising. Keenly observe it and watch how it progresses. For instance, your anger might start as anxiety before turning into an irritation and then progressing to frustration and morphing into full-blown anger. Following your anger as it progresses through all these emotions will make it easier for you to identify the emotions that often precede your anger, which might in turn point you to the underlying issue.

Identify Your Anger Triggers

You should try to identify the specific thoughts or incidents that trigger your anger. If you frequently get angry, you might recognize that there are certain thoughts or incidents that seem to trigger your anger more often. The triggers that frequently trigger your anger might point to one of the three major causes of anger – fear, frustration, or pain. For instance, if your anger is frequently triggered by things such as your friends showing up late or canceling plans, your kids not making their beds, bad traffic, and so on, this shows that the frustration of things not as you expect is the main reason behind your anger problem. From there, you can focus on trying to find out why you get easily frustrated. Similarly, if your anger is frequently triggered by things such as your partner staying out late, the fear of abandonment could be the major reason behind your anger problem.

Sometimes, you might notice that you tend to get angry when you are in a particular environment. For instance, you might notice that you rarely get angry at home, but your irritability seems to be exceptionally high at work. This can be a pointer that you are working in a stress-filled environment which could be the reason behind your anger problem, rather than something about you. In this case, finding another job can help you reduce your likelihood of getting angry.

Keep An Anger Journal

Keeping an anger journal is an effective way of understanding your anger and the reasons behind it. An anger journal is simply a book where you keep a record of your outbursts of anger. Every time you go through a moment of anger, get your journal and record the situation. You should really look deep into yourself and be very honest with yourself when doing this. Write down the incident that triggered your anger, what was happening at that moment, how you were feeling right before it happened, the signs of anger that you felt in your body, the thoughts that accompanied your anger, the intensity of your anger, what you did in reaction to your anger, how other people reacted to your anger, how long you were angry for, how you felt after the anger subsided, whether the issue was resolved or not and so on.

Keeping an anger journal helps you understand the kind of situations and incidents that trigger your anger, your reactions to anger, the thoughts and emotions that accompany your anger and so on. This can give you important clues that will help you uncover any underlying issue behind your anger. When writing your anger journal, it is important to be very detailed. Include each and every little thing pertaining to your anger. In addition, you should avoid judging your feelings when writing your anger journal. The aim here is to gain awareness of your emotions, which will in turn make it easier for you to understand the issues behind the emotions.

Dig Deep by Asking Why

People often have a problem getting to the root of their anger because they only look at it superficially. They don't take the time to dig deeper and question their anger. For instance, if you find yourself upset because your spouse stayed out late, you might tell yourself that you are angry because he stayed out late, which is wrong according to you. However, many will not dig deeper to understand why they think a spouse staying out late is wrong. In order to uncover this, you need to ask yourself several consecutive 'whys'. Below is an example of how you might do this:

I feel so angry right now. Why? Because my husband stayed out late. Why did this offend me? Because I don't know what he was doing out there. Why does this bother me? Because my ex-boyfriend cheated on me, and I am afraid of being cheated on again.

In this case, the endless trail of questions can help you uncover the fact that you are not angry because your husband stayed out late, but because you are afraid of being cheated on again. By digging deeper, you gain more insights about your anger and get to the root of the issues behind your anger. From there, you can focus on addressing the issue rather than the feeling.

Distinguish Between Real And Imagined Anger

Sometimes, the trigger behind your anger is usually a very minor incident. However, your imagination might blow up the incident and trigger an angry reaction that is not proportional to the incident behind the anger. For instance, let's assume you are on your way to work in the morning and you find that there has been an accident that has resulted in a huge traffic snarl up. Since you expected to get to work early, you will naturally feel some annoyance and frustration because of the traffic. However, there is not much you can do about it, and ideally, you would accept the situation and your frustration would subside quickly.

Unfortunately, this is not what happens in most situations. Instead of accepting the situation, your imagination takes over and starts conjuring worst-case scenarios of what might happen because of the traffic snarl up. You imagine meeting your boss on the elevator as you walk into work. You imagine not being able to finish the project you were working on in time for the presentation. You might think of the last time your boss yelled at a colleague for getting to work late. You might even imagine being fired from your job because of your lateness.

By doing this, your imagination blows up the issue out of proportion. Instead of responding to the mild frustration of a traffic jam, your emotions respond to the imagined fear of getting fired from your job. You end up getting enraged and start cussing at the traffic jam. Even after the traffic eases, you continue feeling enraged because of the imagined scenarios playing out in your head.

One key to understanding your anger is to learn to distinguish between real and imagined anger. Whenever you find yourself feeling angry, take a moment to introspect and determine whether your anger is a response to a real situation or an imagined one.

Evaluate The Risk of Mental Health Problems

Sometimes, your anger problem might be result of an underlying psychiatric or psychological disorder. Anger is one of the symptoms of mental disorders such as dissociative identity disorder, obsessive-compulsive disorder, bipolar disorder, and so on. If you find yourself constantly overwhelmed by feelings of anger but you cannot pinpoint any possible reason behind your anger, this could be a sign that there is an underlying medical problem behind your anger. While the possibility of your anger being a result of a medical issue is a lot lower than having an anger management problem, it is better to be sure than sorry. If you are chronically angry without any clue as to why you are constantly feeling angry, it is wise to seek medical or professional opinion to determine whether there is an underlying conditions.

Chapter Summary

- It is important to get to the root of your anger problem in order for you to address the real issue instead of addressing feelings, which are only the symptoms of the problem.

- The first step to understanding your anger is to learn to recognize when you are getting angry and follow the progression of your anger, instead of just taking note of the anger once it has already exploded.

- Keeping an anger journal is also a great way of understand your anger, its triggers, your reactions to it, and the thoughts and emotions that accompany it.

- Asking yourself a series of 'whys' can help you dig deeper and uncover the actual fear or pain behind your anger.

- Sometimes, your anger is a response not to real situations, but to imagined situations created by your mind. Learn to distinguish between real and imagined anger.

- Sometimes, anger might also be a result of an underlying medical condition. If you are chronically angry without any clue as to why you are constantly feeling angry, it might be a good idea to seek the advice of a professional.

In the next chapter, you are going to learn how to let off your anger without hurting others.

Chapter Eight: How To Let Off Your Anger Without Hurting Others

Sometimes, try as you might to prevent getting angry, it is inevitable that something will trigger your anger. In such moments, how you react and deal with your anger determines whether you are in control of your anger or whether your anger is the one controlling you. When you are seething with rage your first impulse might be to react immediately and with violence or aggression. However, reacting aggressively might lead to negative consequences, both for you and people around you. It can damage the relationships between you and others or even lead to loss of a job. While reacting aggressively and exploding is not good, this does not mean that you should bottle up your feelings either. Repressing your anger can also lead to unwanted consequences and make matters worse. In this chapter, we are going to look at some of the steps you can take to constructively and productively deal with your anger, without causing any harm to yourself or others or ruining your relationships.

Before we get to the actual steps you can take to express your anger constructively, you need to note that there are two avenues to dealing with your anger. The first one is behavioral. This avenue focuses on dealing with the physiological basis of your anger. It is concerned with helping you calm down the physiological signs and symptoms of anger that prepare you for a confrontation. The second avenue is cognitive. This one is concerned with helping you gain control over thoughts that might fuel your anger. The steps discussed below will fall under one of these two methods of dealing with anger.

Below are the steps you should take to let off your anger without hurting others:

Watch Out for Signs of Anger

The first step to dealing constructively with your anger is to recognize when you start getting angry and are at risk of letting your emotions loose. Anger is usually accompanied by some physical and emotional signs that prepare you for a confrontation with the target of your anger. By noticing these signs in time, you can start exerting control over your anger before it gets to a point where it feels like you want to explode. The physical signs of anger include clenching your teeth and fists, a pounding heartbeat - this signifies an increase in your heart rate – sweating, especially on the forehead and palms, a knotted stomach, tensed muscles, especially in the region around your neck and shoulders, shaking hands, a flushed face, dizziness, and so on. You can also recognize when you start getting angry by watching your emotions. Some emotional signs that might precede anger include irritation, guilt, fear, sadness, defensiveness, anxiousness, resentment, and so on. People have different reactions to anger, therefore you learn to recognize your unique signs that show you are about to explode.

Stop The Advancement of These Signs

Once you notice any of the above signs of anger, you need to immediately stop them from progressing and try to regain control over your emotions. To do this, you need to stop whatever you were doing that triggered the signs out anger. For instance, if you were arguing with someone, immediately put the argument on hold. Tell the other person that you need a break. If the argument broke out over something crucial you were discussing, assure the person that you will continue the conversation at a later time. Sometimes, it might even be necessary to get away from the vicinity of whatever or whomever triggered your anger for a moment. Calming yourself down is a lot easier when the stimulus of your anger is not in front of you.

Calm Yourself Down

Once you have put a stop to whatever activity that triggered your anger and hopefully stepped away from the thing or person behind your anger, you need to calm yourself down. Remember, when your anger is triggered, your body releases adrenaline and undergoes a number of changes in preparation for the conflict. Part of the purpose of these changes is to ensure that your mind is completely focused on the perceived threat while ignoring else for the moment. In this state of arousal, it can be difficult to think clearly. Therefore, it is important for you to start by calming your body before you focus on calming your mind.

A good way of calming down your body is to take deep breaths. Take a deep breath through your nose to a count of three, hold the breath inside your lungs for a count of three and then breathe out slowly through your mouth to a count of three. Repeat this as many times as necessary until you start calming down. As you breathe, pay attention to other parts of your body that might still be in a confrontational state. For instance, if your fists are clenched, try opening and closing them a few times to help them relax.

Once your body has calmed down from the confrontation state, you can now move on to calming your mind. A good way of doing this is to imagine that your anger is a boiling kettle of water. Try as much as possible to see this kettle within your mind. Then picture yourself switching off the kettle and watching as the water stops bubbling. Picture your anger cooling down just like the kettle of water. Alternatively, you can try to imagine yourself in a calm, peaceful and serene place. You can picture yourself sitting by a lake, walking along a quiet, sandy beach with small waves lapping at your feet, floating on a cloud or taking a walk in the forest. Here is the funny thing about the human mind: the subconscious mind is not very good at telling apart imagined situations from real situations. When you picture yourself in a peaceful place, your subconscious mind will take this to be your actual environment and trigger the good feelings that would come with actually being in such a place.

Reassess The Situation

Once your mind has calmed down, you can now try to go through the situation that triggered your anger more clearly, trying to understand why you got mad and if there is a different perspective to the situation. To do this, you should ask yourself questions like: What did he do or say that really triggered my anger? Was my reaction justified? Could I have made an erroneous assumption that made me react wrongly? Did he really mean what he said? Is this matter really as significant as we are making it seem? Is their view justified? Is there some truth to what he said? Could it be possible he or she was only trying to help me and not to criticize me? Did one of us misunderstand the other?

Remember, anger does not result from a situation, but rather from out interpretation or assessment of the situation. By reassessing the situation and asking yourself the above questions, you might find that there is an alternate way of looking at the situation. Doing this can help you do away with your anger over the situation.

Do Not Express Your Anger Aggressively

When our anger is triggered, most of us are inclined to react aggressively. We feel like yelling at the target of our anger or even hitting them. This is a very destructive way of expressing anger and should be avoided at all costs. Aggressive expression of anger can lead to several negative consequences. It damages relationships, leads to losses when you destroy things to vent your anger, might lead to loss of a job if you act aggressively at work, and can even lead to incarceration if you ever assault a person in a fit of anger. Instead of being aggressive, you should try to communicate your feelings to the other person calmly and respectfully.

Avoid Expressing Your Anger Passively

Some people are not confrontational in nature. Even when they are angry, they do not express their anger directly. The desire for revenge is still there, but instead of confronting the target of their anger, they find other ways to get back at them. For instance, a person might be angry with a colleague, but instead of letting the colleague know they are upset, they might go behind the colleague's back and sabotage his work or spread negative rumors about them in the office. If such a person is angry with the spouse, instead of talking about the issue behind their anger, they will opt for passive ways of expressing their anger, such as not talking to the partner or denying them sex.

On the face of it, this might seem like a better way of expressing anger compared to reacting aggressively. However, passive expression of anger is unhealthy and unproductive for a number of reasons. First, it avoids dealing with the actual problem underlying the anger, which allows the issue to go unresolved, thereby creating room for more anger. Secondly, the person on the receiving end might not understand why the other person is doing things to hurt them, and they might also get angry, creating an even bigger problem. Alternatively, the person on the receiving end of passive anger might show indifference to whatever action is being taken by the angered person. With whatever the angered person is doing not working, their anger can quickly turn into resentment and end up irreparably damaging the relationship between the two.

If you find yourself angry with something or someone, avoid expressing your anger passively. Approach them directly and tell them that you are upset with them and why.

Calmly Express Yourself

Sometimes, it is evident that the other person is wrong. Regardless of how you look at things, it is clear that it is their fault. Even if you feel that your anger is justified, you should restrain yourself from confronting them in the heat of the moment. Resist the temptation to shout at them, either accusing them or demanding for an apology, or to escalate things into a physical confrontation. You should calmly and assertively express your anger to the person you feel has wronged you. Tell them what you are feeling and explain why you are feeling that way. Avoid adopting an accusatory tone, since that will only put the other person on the defensive, making it harder to resolve the issue. Instead, you should communicate your feelings clearly and respectfully.

Keep your focus on what you are feeling and why, instead of focusing on what you think the other person's fault is. You should also avoid being judgmental. For instance, if you are angry with your partner because he or she forgot about the dinner date you had planned to celebrate your anniversary, don't say something like "*You forgot about the dinner date we had planned to celebrate our anniversary! We planned for it since last week! I'm so mad at you! You don't even love me!*" The above statements are focused on what you think is your partner's fault. The statements are accusatory, which is likely to put your partner in a defensive mode. Instead of such statements, you can say something like, "*I am feeling angry because you forgot about the dinner date we had planned to celebrate our anniversary. I am frustrated because we had planned it since last week, and I had been looking forward to it. Can we talk about this?*" The second statements are more respectful and are focused on explaining what you are feeling and why, rather than accusing your partner.

When confronting the target of your anger, you should use specific examples to let them know why you are upset. For example, don't say "*You always forget everything we plan for.*" This will seem like you are out to get them since they know that there are times that they actually remembered and honored your plans. Instead, say something like "*I was upset when you forgot about our dinner date last week.*" This lets the other person clearly understand the particular moment you upset them. They are more likely to apologize or change their ways when you confront them with a specific example instead of stating a general accusation.

Focus On Problem Solving

Getting angry is an indication that there is something wrong and that it needs to be solved. When we feel angry, we perceive the source of our anger as a threat. Instead of focusing on solving the problem, many of us often focus on revenge. We conclude that the other person was trying to hurt us and we therefore decide that we should get back at them. This explains why most arguments are mostly comprised of accusations and name-calling. When you call someone names during an argument, you are basically attacking them instead of telling them why you are upset. This is an unhealthy way of expressing your anger.

The healthy and constructive way of expressing your anger is to focus on solving the problem behind the anger. For instance, if you are angry because one of your employees has been regularly coming to work late, don't approach them angrily threatening to fire them if they don't change their behavior. Instead, wait until you have calmed down, and then call the employee to your office. Talk to him or her and tell them that you are upset because they have been coming to work late. Try to find out why they have been coming in late. If there is a genuine reason behind their tardiness, both of you can then come up with a solution to ensure that they get to work on time or that they compensate for their lateness by leaving the office later to make up the time. If there is no valid reason behind their lateness, just tell them that it is against company policy to get to work late and that you will have no other option but to fire them if they don't change.

Identify The Expectation And Let It Go

This is another great way of constructively dealing with your anger without hurting yourself or others. Many times, our anger is a direct result of the expectations we hold in our minds. We expect people to behave a certain way, we expect that there will be no traffic on our way to work, we expect that the weather will be a certain way, and so on. Most of the time, most of these expectations are irrational because we have little control over external influences. We cannot control other people's behavior. We cannot control traffic. We cannot control the weather. We cannot control a ton of other things we have expectations about. Yet we allow these expectations to trigger our anger.

The solution, therefore, is to try and identify the expectation behind the anger and then let the expectation go. For instance, let's say you are angry because your husband forgot to take out the trash. The first thing you need to do is to acknowledge your anger and the reason behind it. You should tell yourself something like *"I am angry with my husband because he forgot to take off the trash."* Next, you should try and identify what you are trying to achieve. In other words, look for the reason behind your expectation. Why do you want the trash taken out? Maybe you want the trash taken out because you want your house to be clean and tidy. Next, realize your expectation in the situation. In this case, you expected your husband to take out the trash. Finally, let go of the expectation. Instead of getting angry at your husband, you might tell yourself something like "*It's no biggie though, he will take it out later when he gets back.*"

By letting go of the expectation, you are accepting the present as it is. Getting angry about the situation is a resistance to reality, which is irrational. Once you learn to identify and let go of expectations this way, you will be in a better position to deal with your anger in a healthy manner, without hurting yourself or others.

Change Your Thinking Patterns

When you are already feeling angry, it's easy for you to follow into a cycle of negative thoughts that reinforce each other and fuel your anger even more. To avoid falling into this downward spiral, you should try to change your thinking patterns from negative, unhelpful thoughts to more positive ones. For instance, if you are angry because someone has made a costly mistake in your business, it might be easy to think "*we have messed up. This is the end of the road for us.*" Such thoughts only make your situation seem more bleak and will end up making you angrier. Instead of entertaining such thoughts, replace them with thoughts like "*we messed up, but we will recover from this.*" When you tell yourself that there is hope beyond whatever situation you are going through, it becomes easier to let go of your anger.

Move Beyond The Cause of Your Anger

Once something or someone triggers your anger, you might be tempted to keep thinking and brooding about the event; asking yourself why the other person did what they did. However, this does not make things any better. Instead, it might make you even angrier. Once you are done with the situation behind your anger, don't dwell on it. Allow yourself to feel the anger and then accept that whatever happened has already happened and move on from it. For instance, if your partner said something mean to you during an argument, this might make you very angry. However, once you have resolved the argument, do not keep thinking of what your partner said to you. Now that the argument is over and your partner has apologized for their mean words, accept their apology and then move on from what they said about you. If you hold on to it and keep thinking about it, it will only lead to more problems down the road.

Listen To Calming Music

Listening to soothing music can be a perfect way of calming your anger. Listening to music does a number of things that help cool off your anger. Music is generally made to express people's emotions. Listening to soothing music can therefore help you to process your emotions and leave you free from anger. Music also acts as a source of distraction. When listening to music that you like, you focus more on the music than on the things that made you angry. This distraction allows your anger to cool down. If you decide to think about the cause of your anger later, you will approach it from a more clear-headed and rational perspective. Listening to music you like also evokes positive emotions and provides solace after going through a rough time. Next time you find yourself angry about something and feel like you want to explode, grab your iPod and listen to some calming music.

Find Something Funny

Humor is a great way of dealing with and lessening your anger. There are a number of reasons why humor is great for those angry moments. First, injecting humor in an angry situation creates two incompatible mood states. The psychological state of anger is incompatible with the psychological state of finding something funny. You cannot be angry while at the same time find something to be funny. The instant you find something to laugh about, your anger dissipates, and it might even take some effort to go back to the previous angry state.

Secondly, humor provides an alternate way of looking at the anger-inducing situation. Remember, we get angry not because something has happened, but rather because of our judgment of the situation. When we are angry, our thoughts sometimes become unrealistic, irrational, and somewhat silly. Sometimes, all you need to do is to look at the silliness of your thoughts during a moment of anger and that will be enough to get you thinking about the situation in a new and less angering perspective.

Next time you find yourself in an angry situation, try to use humor to diffuse the tense situation. This will cool down your emotions for a moment and allow you to approach the situation from a more rational line of thought. Alternatively, you can find some other funny thing to help you lighten your mood, even if they are not related to the situation. Go online and watch some funny videos. Finding anything to laugh about will reduce your anger by creating the incompatible mood states I mentioned above. If you decide to use humor to diffuse a tense situation, you should avoid sarcastic or cruel humor. Such humor will only fuel your anger and at the same time demean the other person, making the entire situation even worse.

Forgive

Forgiveness is the ultimate method for letting go of your anger. Even if you do everything else recommended in this chapter but fail to forgive the source of your anger, some anger will still remain. Forgiving means totally letting go of any anger, resentment and ill feelings towards the person or the object that caused your anger. Forgiving someone does not mean that accepting that whatever the other person did was right or justified. Instead, it means that you are choosing to not carry that anger with you or hold a grudge against them. You also need to realize that forgiving is not something you do for the other person. You do it for yourself. Carrying anger and resentment can be a huge burden. By choosing to forgive, you are essentially ridding yourself of this burden.

One thing you need to note is that forgiving does not mean that the other person will not hurt you again. If you are worried that the person might do something to anger you again, you should communicate your boundaries to them and let them know that while you have forgiven them, you will not tolerate whatever it is that they did to get you angry in the first place.

Chapter Summary

- How you react and deal with your anger determines whether you are in control of your anger or whether your anger is the one controlling you.

- Expressing your anger aggressively might lead to negative consequences, both for you and people around you.

- There are two methods of dealing with an anger problem – a behavioral and a cognitive approach.

- The first step to dealing constructively with anger is to learn to recognize when you start getting angry by watching out for signs of anger.

- Once you notice the signs of anger, you need to immediately stop them from progressing and overwhelming you with negative emotions.

- Before attempting to calm your mind, you should calm your body. Taking deep breaths is a great way of doing this.

- Once your body has calmed down, you can then calm down your mind by picturing yourself in a peaceful place.

- Once you have calmed down, go through the whole situation again, trying to understand why you got mad and if there is a different perspective to the situation.

- Avoid expressing your anger aggressively or passively. Instead, calmly and assertively express what you feel and the reason behind it.

- When confronting the target of your anger, focus on seeking a solution rather than laying blame on the other person.

- Anger is often caused by expectation. When you find yourself getting angry, try to identify the expectation behind your anger and then let go of the expectation.

- When you find yourself feeling angry, try to change your thinking patterns from negative thoughts to more positive thoughts.

- Don't dwell on the cause of your anger. Deal with your anger and then move on from it.

- Listening to soothing music can help you calm down your anger.

- Humor is another great way of dealing with and lessening your anger.

- Finally, you should learn to forgive. Forgiving means totally letting go of any anger, resentment and ill feelings towards the person or the object that caused your anger. This is the ultimate solution for letting off your anger.

In the next chapter you will learn about some ancient Buddhist secrets that will help you master your emotions and gain control over your anger.

Chapter Nine: Ancient Secrets From Buddhist Monks For Completely Mastering Your Emotions And Dealing With Anger

Buddhism is one of the ancient wisdom traditions of the East that have spent thousands of years studying the human body and mind, with the aim of alleviating human suffering. After centuries of years of self-introspection, observations and experiments, ancient Buddhist monks learned that a lot of human suffering stems from the lack of control over our emotions. They learned that by making some lifestyle tweaks and adopting certain practices, it is possible to master and gain control over our emotions. Today, Buddhist monks are known for their great mastery of their emotions. They don't let their emotions control their actions and behavior. Is there something we can learn from them to help us deal with the emotion of anger?

Despite living in the most advanced era in the history of the earth, the majority of us still have very little control over the workings of our minds. We know so little of what goes on in the small space between our ears. Rather than being in control over our emotions, we are often driven by these emotions, resulting in impulsive actions that we later come to regret. Buddhist monks, in contrast, are finely attuned to the workings of their minds. They have total control over their minds and their emotions, which are creations of the mind. They draw on ancient knowledge and techniques – which were developed over the course of more than 2500 years – to keep at bay the emotional roller coasters many of us go through and achieve a satisfying sense of calmness, awareness, joy and compassion.

The good thing is that by borrowing from this ancient well of knowledge, we can also learn how to exert control over all our emotions, including anger, which was identified by Buddha as one of the three poisons that prevent us from becoming free from suffering. Below are 9 ancient secrets from Buddhist monks that will change the way you think about anger and allow you to regain control over it.

Practice Mindfulness

Mindfulness is an ancient Buddhist practice that involves maintaining a moment-by-moment awareness of everything going on in our bodies and surrounding environment. It involves paying attention to our thoughts, feelings and sensations and accepting them without judging them. When you practice mindfulness, you are in tune with everything happening in the present moment rather than thinking about the future or remembering the past. So, how does this help you deal with anger?

If you have been around angry people, you might have noticed situations where someone was in a rage, yet he insisted that he was not angry. This is a very common occurrence. Many angry people do not want to admit that they are angry. However, this creates a problem. How do they deal with their anger when they won't acknowledge that it is there in the first place?

Buddhist mindfulness teaches that you should acknowledge everything you are feeling, including negative feelings like anger, and then accept them without judging whether they are right or wrong. When you notice yourself feeling angry, don't try to fight, deny, or suppress the anger. Be honest with yourself and recognize that it is there. Don't tell yourself that it is a bad thing to feel angry. Instead, you should say to yourself *"I know I am feeling angry right now. I am angry because this client has not yet deposited money into my account."* By doing this, you acknowledge and embrace your anger, which then makes it easier for you to deal with it.

Use Positive Affirmations And Motivating Self-Talk

Buddhism knows that everything starts from the mind and therefore encourages the use of positive affirmations and motivating self-talk to instill changes in behaviors we want to improve. Affirmations are short, positive statements that you tell yourself with the aim of sparking a change in behavior or beliefs. Our subconscious mind plays an important role in helping us manifest our desires in real life. What we subconsciously believe about ourselves influences our lives. Positive affirmations and motivational self-talk help to reprogram our subconscious minds and create the kind of life we want.

When you use positive affirmations and motivational self-talk in regards to your anger, the aim is to get your subconscious to believe that you do not have an anger problem. Your subconscious mind, in turn, starts reacting to anger-inducing situations with less anger as the belief that you are not an angry person takes root.

Below are some positive affirmations you can use to help you reprogram your subconscious mind and reduce your likelihood of reacting to situations with anger.

- I am a calm and peaceful person.

- I am in control of my emotions.

- I am calm even when in stressful situations.

- I am a forgiving person.

- I am able to recognize and acknowledge my angry feelings without losing my cool.

Accept Everything That Happens

There is a reason why Buddhists put a lot of focus on the mind and not on the outside world. They understood that the mind is the only thing we have total control over. We cannot control the weather. We cannot control our environment. We cannot control other people. Sometimes, we cannot even control our own bodies. Our minds and the thoughts that we allow into it are the only things we can control one hundred percent of the time. The key to living a life that is free of anger, therefore, is to accept that we have no control over everything else and to accept everything that happens as it is. Without acceptance, you cannot rid yourself of anger.

Acceptance does not mean that you should become indifferent or apathetic. It means that you should make peace with the fact that something has happened and that there is nothing you can do to change it. Instead of being bitter or creating negativity out of the situation, you should focus on the next course of action. If someone cuts you off in traffic, the deed is done and there is nothing you can do it. Getting angry will not undo it. Instead of becoming bitter about it, accept that it is done and then focus on what you need to do next. If your spouse cheats on you, you cannot undo it either. What you need to do is to accept that he or she has done it, accept that you are feeling angry because of that, and then focus on the next course of action – do you forgive them or do you end the relationship? Once you learn to accept things as they are, you will have gained a great deal of power over your anger and bitterness.

Recognize That Anger Is Not Real

Have you ever stopped to think about where your anger comes from? When we get angry, we tend to think of our anger as something that comes to infect as from inside. However, Buddhists will tell you that no one and nothing has the power to make you angry. Anger is something you do to yourself. All emotions, including anger, are more than direct biological responses to external stimuli. Instead, emotions are a response to the thoughts that we think about these external stimuli. Before an external stimulus is translated into an emotion, it first gets filtered through the memories, biases, interpretations, judgments and thoughts that we hold in our minds. Everything you experience in life is not the reality, but rather your own version of reality.

There is a common story in Buddhism about a father whose son went to work in a foreign country. The son had been abroad for over ten years, during which time he had not seen or communicated with his father. One day, a man comes from the foreign country and tells the father that his son just died. After hearing the news, the father is overcome by grief. However, considering that he had not spoken with his son for over 10 years, he had no way of knowing whether his son was alive all those years. The son could have died a year after going abroad, yet the father only felt grief after receiving the news. A while later, word comes that the messenger was lying. The son is still alive. Without seeing or communicating with his son, the man's grief dissipates and he is filled with happiness. In all this, the father's emotions went from indifference to grief to happiness, yet nothing had changed. The only thing that had changed was his thoughts about his son.

This story shows that when you experience something, you are not actually experiencing it outside of yourself, but rather inside your mind. What appears one way to you will appear a different way to another person. Therefore, even the mental states you experience, such as anger, sadness, happiness, grief, and so on are constructs of your mind. They are not real. They are like shadows. They disappear when you shine a light on them. Allowing ourselves to be controlled by our emotions, therefore, is like allowing ourselves to be controlled by shadows. Next time you are feeling overwhelmed by feelings of anger, you should remind yourself that the anger is not real, that it has only been created by your mind. Once you realize that it is not real, you are less likely to do something dangerous or damaging out of anger.

Think Lightly of Yourself And Deeply of Others

Have you ever wondered why Buddhist monks are so committed to learning about the world and the mind and a ton of other ancient knowledge? The monks do it not for their own gain, but so that they can use the knowledge and enlightenment to help others live better lives. They are willing to spend their entire lives in isolation and away from material comforts for the sake of humanity. Adopting the same kind of selflessness shown by Buddhist monks might be the key to dealing with your anger issues.

A lot of times, anger is usually a result of an excessive focus on the self. People tend to get angry when they feel like something about them is being threatened. Their wants and desires, their ego, their expectations, their insecurities, their belongings, and so on. If you want to gain control over your anger, you should adopt the selfless attitude shown by Buddhist monks. You should focus less on yourself and your problems and more on helping other people with their problems.

Remember The Impermanence of Life

We live in a society that is scared of death. We don't like thinking or talking about death. Anything associated with death makes us uneasy. We use words like "pass on" and "expire" to avoid mentioning the word "die". We treat death as an abstract concept that only happens to the old and the sick. However, death is a reality of life and we should spend more time thinking about it. Why am I talking about death? How is it related to anger?

Thinking about death and the impermanence of life helps to give us some perspective. When we remember that life is not permanent and that we will die one day, we stop placing too much importance to some minor things that would normally irk us. Once you consider that you won't be here forever, it suddenly doesn't matter whether someone squeezes the toothpaste tube from the middle or if they are late meeting up with us. It's not that these minor things stop annoying you. Instead, you realize that they are not worth getting worked over. If today was your last day on earth, would you worry about the jerk who cuts you off in traffic? Highly unlikely. Instead, you would be focused on enjoying your last few hours on earth. Next time you feel yourself getting worked up over minor issues, ask yourself whether it will matter when you are on your deathbed. If it won't, then there is probably no point getting worked up over it.

Contemplate The Opposite

Like Buddha once said, you cannot fight anger with anger. Anger can only be fought with non-anger. The Buddhist principle of contemplating the opposite is deeply rooted in psychology. Our minds cannot hold two opposing thoughts or emotions at the same time. You cannot be happy and angry at the same time. You cannot feel like shouting at someone and at the same time be patient with them. Therefore, whenever you feel yourself starting to get angry, you should start contemplating an emotion that is the complete opposite of your anger. For instance, you might think about a time in the past when you were extremely happy. By merely thinking about a time you were happy, your anger will start subsiding.

Learn To Reanalyze The Situation

When you are enraged, your anger can often feel like a good thing. It looks like a guardian angel that has come to help you out on the battlefield and protect you from getting hurt or exploited. When such thoughts are running through your mind, they fuel your anger and make it feel justified. Exerting control over your anger when you have the illusion that anger is a friend can be quite difficult. However, the truth is that uncontrolled anger is not our friend or protector. Instead, it is an enemy that destroys our personal and professional relationships, affects our health and leads to stress and depression.

When you notice signs of anger in yourself, don't be in a rush to encourage them, regardless of how justified you might feel. Take the time to reassess the situation rationally and recognize your anger as an emotion that might be up to no good. Instead of entertaining and encouraging the anger, think of other ways you can resolve the situation without resorting to anger.

Use Meditation To Control Your Anger

When most people think of Buddhism, they automatically think of meditation. This is because meditation is one of the core tenets of Buddhism. Meditation trains you to focus your mind and gain control over your thoughts. Considering that all emotions – including anger – stem from our thoughts, gaining control over your thoughts through meditation can be a great way of learning how to control your anger, both in the short and the long-term. Meditation can help you manage your anger in a number of ways. During meditation, you are required to focus your mind on something like your breath and clear away other thoughts from your mind. When faced with irritants and stressors during your day to day life, you can use the same skill to focus your mind and gain control over any negative thoughts that might be fueling your anger. This skill acts as a buffer between your feelings of anger and any impulsive action you might be tempted to take.

Meditation also gives you a deep sense of calmness and inner peace, thereby increasing your overall tolerance to stressors and making you less likely to explode aggressively when you find yourself in anger-inducing situations. Once you start meditating regularly, you will notice that you will start becoming angry less often and your anger will become less intense.

Finally, regular meditation also enhances the neural connections in the part of your brain known as the prefrontal cortex. This is the part of the brain that is responsible for self-awareness and regulation of social behavior. This means that when you regularly practice meditation, you will have a better sense of self-control. In addition, meditation unbinds your conscious mind from the senses, giving you the ability to observe things without impulsively reacting to them. This is why meditation is a greatly recommended practice for people dealing with anger problems.

Chapter Summary

- Buddhist monks have managed to master and gain control over their emotions, and it is possible for us to also gain control over our emotions, including anger, by borrowing from some of their knowledge and practices.

- Practice mindfulness to acknowledge and gain awareness of your anger. Without acknowledging your anger problem, it becomes impossible to deal with it.

- Use positive affirmations and motivating self-talk to reprogram your subconscious mind to respond calmly to anger-inducing situations.

- Instead of trying to control everything and fighting things that go contrary to your expectations, learn to accept everything that happens and you will be less likely to become angry over things that are not within your control.

- Recognize that anger is not real. It is a construct of your mind. Instead of letting your anger control you, you can overcome it by changing your thoughts about the situation.

- Focus more on helping others rather than focusing on yourself and your needs.

- Remember the impermanence of life. Focus on enjoying and savoring life rather than letting minor issues to rob you of your peace of mind.

- Avoid the temptation to fight fire with fire. When faced with anger, contemplate an opposite feeling like happiness and patience.

- When you are angry, anger can feel like a good thing. Learn to reanalyze the situation and see anger for what it is – a strong emotion that might drive you to rash, unwanted actions if you do not bring it under control.

- Use Buddhist meditation to control your anger problem and achieve a deep sense of calmness and inner peace.

In the next chapter, you are going to learn about some great tips you can use to resolve conflicts in your family without resorting to anger.

Chapter Ten: Tips For Resolving Conflict In Your Family

Conflicts are a natural part of human interactions, since it is impossible for two or more people to be in agreement about all matters, all the time. This means that conflicts are inevitable any place where there is more than one person, including at home. Conflicts within the family are some of the most intense, mostly because the people closest to us are the ones we tend to show our realest selves and our realest emotions. If a person has an anger management problem, the family is the first relationship that gets affected by the anger issue. At the same time, family members could be the triggers behind a person's anger. While conflicts are inevitable, it is important to ensure that they are resolved in a healthy manner to avoid destroying the important relationships we share with our family members. In this chapter, we are going to look at tips on how to resolve family conflicts without resorting to anger.

Acknowledge And Embrace Conflict

One of the biggest problems that makes matters difficult in the family is avoidance of conflict. When something happens, some people might opt to pretend that nothing happened in order to prevent the confrontation that comes with conflict. This not only keeps the issue from being resolved, but also leads to resentment, which can have very negative consequences to the relationship. The key, therefore, is to acknowledge that there is a conflict and embrace it. Only by doing this will you be able to work on resolving the conflict. This should be done the moment the problem is noticed, since the more it remains unaddressed, the more it will get entangled with other issues.

Set Time To Address The Conflict

Once you notice that there is a conflict, you need to set up a time and place where you can discuss the problem for an adequate amount of time without getting interrupted. You should avoid interruptions because not only will they prevent the resolution of the conflict, but an interruption might cause you to abandon the talk at a point where there was a misunderstanding about the conflict, thus making matters even worse. Unless there is no other way to go about it, avoid trying to resolve issues through text messages. Texts leave a lot of room for misunderstanding, which can make matters even worse. Once it is time to discuss the problem, each person should be given enough time to say what they need to say. However, do not try to monopolize or control the conversation, and neither should your partner. Both of you should be allowed to share your views and feelings about the situation.

Listen To Understand, Not To Respond

Many times, resolving a conflict becomes difficult because no one is listening to the other. If you are listening just so that you can respond, misunderstandings are bound to happen, making the situation even worse. As your partner shares their feelings and views, you should listen carefully to understand what exactly they are feeling. Don't interrupt them until they are done speaking. During the conversation, try to keep your emotions at bay.

If there is something you don't understand about what your partner is saying, ask questions so that they can clarify issues for you. Avoid asking sarcastic questions or questions that may be seen as accusatory, since this will only lead to a shouting match. Even if you are not satisfied with their answers, avoiding jeering or losing your temper.

The aim here is to make sure that you have the full story. Very often, conflicts arise from the fact that we don't have all the information about a situation. Instead of seeking more facts, we then make up assumptions to fill in the blanks. These assumptions are wrong and biased most of the time. By listening carefully to your partner and asking questions where things are not clear, you are in a better position to resolve the conflict because you have the full story.

Consider Things From Your Partner's Perspective

Conflicts arise because one or both of you believe that some of their needs are not being met. Very often, people bring this view with them to the negotiating table. They don't try to understand the other person's perspective. They believe they are right and the other person is wrong. This is a very ineffective approach when you are trying to solve a conflict.

The key to resolving a conflict is to consider things from your partner's perspective. Put yourself in his or her shoes and put your judgments and biases aside, if only for a moment. Try to understand why the reason behind their views and opinions. What are his or her needs? For instance, if a couple is arguing about the husband spending too much time at work, both of them will have very different approaches to the problem. For the husband, spending too much time at work might seem justified because he wants to get that promotion that will make it possible for the couple to afford their dream home. The wife, on the other hand, might think that by spending too much time at work, the husband does not love her and is avoiding her. Without looking at things from each other's perspective, it might be difficult for them to resolve the issue. The husband might wrongly assume that the wife wants to sabotage their dreams, while the wife wrongly assumes that the husband does not love her anymore.

When putting yourself in your partner's shoes, you should not stop at trying to understand the reason behind their views, opinions and feelings. You should also try to understand how their views, opinions and feelings might affect their interpretation of your own words and actions. Once both of you can do this, you will be in a better position to understand and resolve the problem.

Take A Break If Necessary

When discussing an uncomfortable issue, it is not always possible to keep emotions in check. Your partner might say or do something and get your tempers flaring. If you feel yourself starting to get worked up, it might be a good idea to take a break to recompose yourself before continuing with the negotiations. This will prevent you from losing your cool and impulsively doing something that will make matters even worse. If you find it impossible to calm yourself down in a moment and continue with the conversation, talk to your partner and ask to finish the conversation another time. When doing this, make it clear to him or her that you are not running away from the conversation. Assure him or her that you will return to the conversation once you have managed to get a hold of yourself and resolve the issue.

Focus On The Problem, Not The Person

One of the biggest mistakes most people make when addressing a conflict is to focus their anger on their partner. You need to remember that you are there to solve the problem. It should be a case of you and your partner against the problem, not you versus your partner. Therefore, once you sit down to discuss the problem, don't try to lay the blame on your partner. Don't try to shame or guilt your partner into agreeing with you. This might work in the short term, but it will lead to bigger problems in the long run.

To keep your focus on the problem, you should discuss events and behaviors that you do not like, rather than your partner's personality. For instance, say something like *"I don't like it when we are late for church"*, rather than "*You don't know how to keep time.*" When talking about things that annoy you, you should talk about specific incidents instead of generalizing. You should also avoid using the words "*always*" and "*never*". These words are typically used to generalize behaviors and will only get your partner on the defensive. Another good idea is to use "*I*" statements, rather than "*you*" statements. This way, you let your partner know what you don't like or approve of instead of accusing him or her based on what you think they are doing wrong.

In your conversation, try as much as possible to remain civil and polite. Avoid calling your partner names, picking at his or her insecurities or attacking them in any other way. If you feel yourself getting worked up to the extent that you are tempted to do this, it is best to step away for a moment to cool yourself down.

Maintain Your Focus

Another major problem that many couples make when trying to resolve problems is to bring up other problems from the past. For instance, a couple might be trying to resolve an argument about who should do the dishes, only for one of them to bring up an old argument about who is supposed to take out the trash or cook the meals. Doing this will only sidetrack you from the current conflict and raise other conflicts that should have been done with in the first place. To avoid this, make sure that you maintain your focus on the issue at hand. If you had discussed and resolved an issue before, let it remain in the past.

Pick Your Battles

Conflicts are not easy. They drain you of energy and fill you with negativity. Therefore, before getting into an argument with your significant other, it is worth taking a moment to consider whether this is an issue that you should really be fighting about. Very often, many couples fight very minor issues. Of course, when left unaddressed, these little things can blow up and lead to a lot of stress within the family. Here, I am not suggesting that you should avoid bringing something up even when it annoys you. Instead, you should consider whether the matter is something worth getting worked up over. For instance, your partner might be headed to the mall and you ask him or her to bring you a box of chocolates or a can of beer from the mall. Unfortunately, your partner forgets about it. Would it really be worth it to become upset with your partner and get into a full blown argument because of something so trivial?

Focus On Conflict Resolution, Not Winning The Argument

Here is the thing with anger; when you are angry, you tend to feel that you are right and the other person is wrong. Sometimes, people carry this view with them when addressing the conflict. This can be problematic. When you approach the conflict resolution process with the view that you are right and your partner is wrong, your objectives for the negotiation might be very different. Instead of trying to resolve the conflict, you go into the conversation with the aim of getting your partner to agree with your point of view. For instance, if you feel that they are wrong, you might want them to admit their guilt and therefore apologize to you. If your partner is complaining about something and you feel that you did nothing wrong, your aim might be to convince them that you did nothing wrong and get them to drop their complaint. Unfortunately, it can be difficult to resolve the issue if your aim is to win the argument rather than make the situation better. To avoid this, approach the conversation with an open mind and focus on reconciliation and ensuring that the needs of both of you are met, not just your needs.

Find Solutions That Meet The Needs of Both Of You

Once both of you have shared your concerns and understood what the actual problem is, try to come up with solutions that meet the needs of both of you. Both of you might have serious concerns, therefore it is good to note that an effective solution might require both of you to compromise on something. Avoid getting into a competition to see who will give up less. Instead, the focus should be on ensuring that both of you are satisfied with the solution. It is also good to keep in mind that it will not always be possible for both of you to compromise. Some situations might require one of you to forego getting your way. The key here is to keep an open mind and focus on coming up with the best solution, even it might require a bit of sacrifice on your part.

Request Behavior Change Only

Another thing that makes it difficult for couples to resolve conflicts is situations where one partner asks the other to change something that is a part of their identity. For instance, let us assume that you are an introvert who loves spending time at home while your partner is an extrovert who loves going out and interacting with people. You are arguing because you feel that your partner does not spend enough time with you because he or she loves going out on weekends when you are supposed to be spending time together. In such a situation, asking your partner to stop being extroverted won't work. You are essentially asking him or her to change who they are. If you feel that a conflict can only be resolved through some change on your partner's part, you should only request them to change their behavior. Avoid asking them to change their attitudes, beliefs and feelings or asking them to be different, because this will feel like an attack on who they are. If you want them to drop certain behaviors, suggest a compromise like spending every other weekend at home together.

Be Ready To Forgive

This is the final part of resolving a conflict. Once you have discussed the issue and come up with solutions, now is the time to let the issue go. If your partner had indeed done something wrong, forgive them. If you had done something wrong, apologize to your partner. Forgiving means that you have accepted the proposed solution, and that you won't hold any more anger towards your partner because of the same issue unless it is repeated. Once you forgive, don't bring up the issue again, even if you find yourself in a similar argument in future. Don't claim to have forgiven your partner if you feel that the issue has not been resolved satisfactorily since this will only lead to resentment and grudges.

Chapter Summary

- A person's family are the first to get affected by the person's anger problem, and therefore it is important for one to learn to resolve conflicts in the family without resorting to anger.

- The first part of resolving a family conflict is to acknowledge that the conflict exists.

- You should set up a tie and place to discuss the problem. Avoid trying to resolve conflicts over text.

- When having a conversation to resolve a conflict, listen to understand, not to respond.

- Considering things from your partner's perspective will help you understand their needs and concerns.

- If you start getting worked up during the conversation, take a break to calm yourself down.

- During the conversation, focus on the problem, not the person.

- Don't bring up issues from the past. Focus on the problem at hand.

- Conflicts are not easy. Avoid getting worked up over minor issues.

- When addressing a conflict, focus on finding a solution to the problem, rather than winning the argument.

- Try to come up with solutions that meet the needs of both of you. This might require both of you to compromise or sacrifice something.

- Don't ask your partner to change anything that forms part of their identity such as beliefs, attitudes and feelings. Only request for behavior change.

- Finally, if you are trying to find a solution to a conflict with your family, you should be ready to forgive.

In the next chapter, you are going to learn how to let go of grudges.

Chapter Eleven: How To Let Go Of Grudges

There are people who have a lot of trouble letting go of their anger. When someone does something to hurt them, they are overwhelmed by feelings of anger, sadness and confusion, especially if they were hurt by someone they loved and trusted. Such a person might have trouble expressing their anger, and they might therefore try to suppress the anger even though they are hurting deep down. They start feeling resentment, vengeance and hostility towards the person behind their anger and convince themselves that they are the victims in this situation. This resentment grows into a grudge that stays around for years, sometimes even lifetimes. The mere thought of someone you hold a grudge against triggers a deep anger in you. Once anger turns into a grudge, it can be hard to let the go of the anger, even if you have a strong desire to let go of it.

When someone develops a grudge, their anger, resentment and bitterness are usually directed towards the source of their hurt. They feel that holding a grudge is a way of punishing the person who hurt them. Unfortunately, grudges do the complete opposite. Instead of punishing the perceived wrongdoer, they do more damage to the grudge-holder. Holding a grudge is like carrying around a bag of toxic waste. Grudges are painful to maintain. They keep your wounds open and keep alive the pain of things that happened a long time ago. They transform your anger into an unhealthy force that takes a mental and physiological toll on you. Grudges zap your energy and cause negative impacts on your health and well-being. The anger and bitterness from holding grudges can also hinder your ability to form and enjoy new relationships.

Clearly, grudges harm you more than they do the person against whom you hold the grudge. So, the question is, how do you let grudges go and rid yourself of this toxic, unexpressed anger?

Acknowledge Your Feelings

The first step of dealing with any negative feeling is to acknowledge that you are experiencing the feeling. It is impossible for you to let go of your grudge until you accept that it is there and try to understand how it makes you feel. Take a deeper look into your grudge. What offense did the other person commit? What are the emotions behind your anger? In most cases, anger will be the strongest emotion behind the grudge. However, there is a high chance that it is not alone. Grudges are also usually fueled by feelings of resentment, jealousy, envy, sadness and frustration. While these emotions might not be as strong as anger, they play a huge role in keeping the grudge alive. It is important to be very honest with yourself at this point. Whatever emotion you discover, don't deny or ignore it. If you deny or ignore any of these emotions, you won't be able to release it and therefore let go of your grudge.

Once you have identified the feelings and emotions behind your grudge, the next step is to make a conscious choice to let them go. For instance, you might allow yourself to feel angry for the next one hour, and then completely let go of the feeling of anger after the hour is over and forget about it forever. Here, you need to understand one thing. Grudges usually come with an identity. A grudge makes you identify yourself as a victim. This identity gives you some kind of strength and purpose and justifies your anger. Therefore, letting go of a grudge might feel like you are losing a part of you. Don't let this deter you, because you know you are doing it to make yourself better. Once you successfully let go of a grudge, you can then fill any void left by the grudge with a more positive identity.

Share Your Feelings

Grudges usually form as a result of unexpressed anger. People form grudges because they feel misunderstood, unheard, they are not believed, and so on. In this case, it might be necessary to share your feelings with someone and become heard in order to be able to let the grudge go. Once you have acknowledged and identified your feelings as described in the previous step, look at the feelings and decide whether you can handle them by yourself or if you need to share them with someone else.

If you decide to share the feelings, you have two options. You can either share them with the person you hold the grudge against or with a different person that you can trust. If you decide to share the feelings with the person against whom the grudge is leveled, it is important to keep the conversation objective. Don't attack or accuse them. Instead, simply tell them what you are feeling and the reasons behind the feelings. The person might decide to share their side of the story after hearing you out, and that's okay.

If you decide to share the feelings with a close confidante, make sure that the person cares about you but still has the ability to remain objective. Some friends, in a bid to not hurt you, might end up validating or reinforcing your feelings, which is something you want to avoid at this point. Similarly, your family already have a natural bias towards you and might be inclined to justify your feelings. You want someone will look at the issue without any bias or judgment. If you don't have friends or family members who can remain objective, it might be wise to talk to a counselor or therapist. Sharing your feelings with someone, whether the person involved, a close friend or any other trusted confidante will release the pent-up tension and make it easier for you to let go of the negative emotions.

Let Bygones Be Bygones

Grudges are rarely rational. They do not help in any way. They don't make the other person pay for their perceived wrongs in any way. Sometimes, the person might not even be aware that you have a grudge against them. Instead, the grudge only zaps your energy and fills you with negative energy that affects your life and makes it hard for you to enjoy new moments. This shows that holding onto a grudge is of no use. Therefore, once you have acknowledged and explored your feelings and hopefully shared the feelings with someone, it is time to let the grudge go. The incident behind the grudge happened in the past. Let it stay there. Avoid thinking too much about it or discussing it, since this will only make it harder for you to get over it. Focus on the present and the future and let the past be. If someone happens to bring the incident up in a conversation, either change the topic or treat it as something that happened in the past that has no bearing on your present.

Put Yourself In Their Shoes

Putting yourself in the other person's shoes and trying to understand the reason behind their actions is also an important part of letting go of a grudge. People do not always do things out of malice. Sometimes, there are some other extraneous circumstances behind their actions. Perhaps the person was going through a difficult time. Perhaps they were not even aware that whatever they did hurt you in any way. There being other circumstances behind their actions does not necessarily justify whatever they did to hurt you. However, looking at things from their perspective helps you to understand that they did not do whatever they did with the deliberate aim of hurting you, and this can make it easier for you to let go of the grudge.

Be Patient

Letting go of a grudge is not an easy process, especially if it is a grudge you have held for a long time. Like I mentioned earlier, a grudge becomes part of your identity, and letting go of it can feel like you are trying to change part of who you are. Therefore, once you have decided to let go of your grudge, you should be patient with yourself. Understand that healing is a process that might take some time. Don't give up on the healing process once you see that it has been several days and the feelings of hurt and anger have not dissipated. Feelings that you have carried for years cannot always be undone in a few days. Trust in the process with the confidence that once it is done, you will no longer carry around any hurt and negativity

Forgive

Grudges are the direct result of not forgiving. Someone does something, and instead of forgiving them, you decide to carry the hurt with you for the rest of your life. Therefore, you have to forgive to be able to let go of the grudge. Many people have a problem with forgiving because they think it makes them vulnerable to go through the hurt again. However, forgiving does not mean excusing their behavior or forgetting what the other person did. Forgiving means acknowledging that the other person did something to hurt you but then choosing to let go of the anger and bitterness you feel. You are still aware of what they did, and if need be, you are taking any necessary action to protect yourself from being hurt by them in future.

However, you are choosing to let feelings about the past remain in the past.

You should also keep in mind that when you choose to forgive, you are not doing it for the person who hurt you. You are doing it for yourself. Holding a grudge is an emotional burden that takes a huge toll on your health and your happiness. By forgiving, you are ridding yourself of this burden and allowing yourself to enjoy life without being encumbered by negative emotions from the past. You do not even need to tell the person who hurt you that you have forgiven them. You are simply choosing not to hold the person in debt and letting go of the anger, the hurt and the bitterness for your own sake.

Chapter Summary

- Grudges are a result of the resentment, vengeance and hostility that crop up when anger is not expressed.

- While grudges are directed towards the perceived wrongdoer, they do more damage to the person holding the grudge that to the wrongdoer.

- The first step of dealing with a grudge is to acknowledge that you have a grudge and examine the emotions that are behind the grudge.

- Since grudges are a result of unexpressed anger, seeking an audience and sharing your feelings can help you let go of your anger.

- Once you decide to let go of a grudge, don't dwell on it. Allow the past to remain where it belongs – in the past.

- Putting yourself in the other person's shoes can help you understand the reasons behind their actions, therefore making it easier for you to let go of the grudge.

- Healing is a process that takes time, especially if you have held the grudge for a long time. Don't be in a rush. Be patient with yourself and give time to the process.

- Finally, you should be ready to forgive. Forgiving does not mean forgetting what the other person did or excusing their actions. Instead, it means choosing not to hold them in debt for what they did.

In the next chapter, you are going to learn about factors that may exacerbate your anger problem.

Chapter Twelve: Factors That May Exacerbate Your Anger Problem

An anger problem already takes a huge toll on your physical and mental well-being and affects other things such as your personal and professional relationships, your self-esteem, your safety, your judgment, and so on. Therefore, it is important to take action to bring your anger under control. Sometimes, however, there are other factors that might exacerbate your anger problem. Dealing with an anger problem without being aware of these factors might become more challenging because you might be engaging in activities that end up sabotaging your efforts. In this chapter, we take a look at some of the factors that might be fueling your anger problem.

Alcohol Use

If you have an anger problem, alcohol might not be good for you. Alcohol and anger are like two evil twins. Alcohol fuels your anger and often leads to displays of aggressive behavior, while anger and frustration often lead a person to seek refuge in the bottle, creating a vicious cycle that can be hard to escape from.

There are a number of reasons why alcohol is not good for you if you have an anger problem. First, alcohol gives you tunnel vision. When you are drunk, your ability to analyze information from multiple environmental sources is compromised. This, in turn, has an impact on your ability to correctly judge the intentions behind the behaviors and actions of people you interact with. For instance, let's assume you are at the bar with your partner. You have already downed a couple of drinks. An acquaintance of your partner's, who is seated a few tables away, sees your partner, smiles and waves. If you had not been drinking, you would take a moment to assess the situation and conclude that they probably know each other and that the gesture is a harmless greeting to an acquaintance. When drunk, however, your ability to analyze the situation, as well as your reasoning, is compromised. When drunk, you might view the harmless greeting as an attempt on the other person's part to flirt with your partner, and are a lot more likely to respond to the situation aggressively.

Second, alcohol brings out aggression in people. Alcohol is a depressant. It slows down the activity in the prefrontal cortex. This is the part of the brain that is responsible for self-awareness, regulation of social behavior and control over impulses. Therefore, when you are drunk, you are more likely to give in to the impulsive actions that are usually associated with anger, such as acting physically or verbally aggressive towards someone who angers you. For people who normally express their anger outwardly, alcohol turns up the intensity with which they express their anger. People who normally suppress their anger are also more likely to express it when tipsy. A study conducted by a professor from Brown University's Center For Alcohol and Addiction found that when intoxicated, people who normally tend to suppress their feelings of anger are 5% more likely to engage in violence.

Alcohol also reduces a person's ability to think about the long-term impacts of their actions. When drunk, you tend to worry less about the possible consequences of aggressive behavior. When sober, if someone angers you, you might be tempted to punch them in the face or take some other aggressive action. However, the fear that you might hurt the person, get hurt yourself or even get arrested holds you back from aggression. Alcohol reduces the significance of the consequences of your aggressive behavior. You are not worried about hurting the other person or getting arrested, either because you do not take the time to consider that it might happen, or because you don't care anyway.

Finally, social and cultural factors are also more tolerant to aggression when it is accompanied by drunkenness. Research by the Norwegian Institute For Alcohol And Drug Research and the Swedish Institute For Social Research shows that the likelihood of people engaging in aggressive behavior increases both after they have drunk an alcoholic drink, as well as after drinking a non-alcoholic placebo drink when they were lead to believe that the drink was alcoholic. In other words, people tend to get more aggressive when they think they are drunk, even when they are actually sober. This happens because society is more tolerant to aggressive behavior by drunk people. Therefore, a person with an anger problem might take alcohol as a mask for expressing their aggression, since they know that their aggression will be more tolerated and is more likely to be forgiven when it is displayed under the cover of drunkenness.

Drug Abuse

Just like alcohol, drugs are highly interdependent with anger. Drugs intensify an anger problem, while an anger problem leads to increased drug abuse, forming a highly dangerous combination. People who have trouble dealing with or expressing their anger might often resort to drug abuse as an escape from their feelings. For instance, someone who has undergone a traumatic experience, such as sexual assault or losing a loved one might feel angry but have no proper channel of expressing their anger. Such a person might turn to drug abuse as a way of coping with their anger. Alternatively, someone who has trouble expressing anger because of self-esteem issues might turn to drug abuse. Such a person might find that they have no trouble expressing their anger when they are high, since they do not care about the feelings of others or societal expectations when high. Unfortunately, drug abuse often leads to unhealthy ways of dealing with and expressing anger, thereby making the anger problem even worse.

Sometimes, a person's anger problem might be fueled by the family problems stemming from their use of the drug. When a person starts abusing drugs, it often leads to conflicts in the family. The person might start neglecting the family or misusing money to sustain their addiction, thus leading to conflicts which might make a person perpetually angry. The person's guilt because of their use of drugs might also lead to anger. The anger might also be an unwanted symptom of the drug's effect on the brain.

Alternatively, the anger might be a withdrawal symptom when the person is unable to access the drug.

Anger can also make it hard for a person to break their addiction. After turning to drug abuse as a way of expressing their anger, such a person might have no other healthy way of coping with their anger. If the person was already recovering from substance abuse, experiencing feelings of anger and frustration can easily lead to relapse since the person has not learned other healthy ways of expressing their anger. Most of these people turn to drugs because they might feel that these drugs soothe their disturbing thoughts and calm down the angry impulses that might be firing inside their minds.

Marijuana is one of the drugs that is highly appealing for people with an anger problem, mostly because of its sedating effect that makes them feel relaxed and at ease. Unfortunately, studies show that use of marijuana can make an anger problem worse in the long run. Other drugs that are usually associated with anger problems include cocaine, meth, benzodiazepines and anabolic steroids. It is important to note that it is virtually impossible to deal with an anger management problem when a person uses drugs frequently. The person first needs to stop their addiction in order to be able to deal with their anger problem.

Negative Thoughts

Sometimes, an anger problem might also be exacerbated by negative thoughts. Some people have a pessimistic state of mind. Their minds are filled with negative thoughts which in turn distort their view of the world, creating a cycle where negative thoughts lead to a negative view of life, which leads to negative emotions, which in turn lead to negative behaviors that reinforce the negative thoughts. One example of a negative thinking pattern that often exacerbates anger problems is something known as black and white thinking. If you have black and white thinking, you tend to divide people, things or situations into two categories, without considering that most people, things and situations exist on a spectrum.

For instance, if you come home and realize that there are unwashed dishes on the kitchen sink, you might automatically conclude that your spouse is a lazy person. You do not take the time to consider whether your spouse had a busy day and had not gotten around to washing the dishes. There is even a chance that your spouse was not feeling well and therefore could not clean the dishes. In your dualistic thinking, you might find it hard to believe that a person would leave dirty dishes on the sink unless they are lazy. Instead of trying to find out why your spouse did not clean the dishes, you just get angry and start calling them lazy.

Dealing with your anger problem when you have such a negative thinking pattern can be challenging and ineffective. Once you notice that you have negative or irrational thinking patterns, you should make an attempt to reprogram your thoughts to a more positive pattern. Accept the fact that no one is perfect. If you keep dividing people and situations into good or bad, lazy or hardworking, love or hate, and so on, you are going to have very high expectations which will only lead to frustration and anger. You should also learn to focus more on the positive than the negative. For instance, instead of focusing on the fact that your spouse forgot to take out the trash, focus on the fact that they did mow the lawn and clean the garage.

Beliefs

Your anger problem might also be fueled by your belief system. A person's beliefs are the things the person holds to be true. Beliefs are the guiding principles that determine what is important to you. Our values, attitudes, behaviors, thoughts and decisions are usually based on our beliefs. For instance, if you believe that it is wrong for people to take advantage of others, you might avoid all actions that require you to take advantage of another person. Your belief system starts forming during your childhood and is usually instilled by your parents and teachers, while others are learned through observation.

While beliefs play an important role in guiding our behaviors and thinking processes, our beliefs can also lead to problems. For instance, if you believe that you should always get your way, you are more likely to feel frustrated and angry if something does not go your way. If you believe that smart people cannot get deceived, you are more likely to feel stupid and angry at yourself if someone deceives you. You are essentially blaming yourself for another person's dishonesty, which is not within your control. If you believe that everybody needs to hold you in high regard, you are more likely to feel angry if someone treats you with indifference.

If you realize that you have an anger problem, you should take a look at your belief system and try to identify if there are some underlying irrational beliefs behind your anger. Once you identify the irrational beliefs, you can then make some adjustments to the beliefs as a way of calming yourself down. For instance, instead of believing that you should always get your way, you should tell yourself that your value as a person remains intact even if things don't go your way. Instead of believing that smart people cannot get deceived, you should tell yourself that another person's dishonesty does not make you stupid. Instead of the belief that everyone should hold you in high regard, tell yourself that you do not need the acceptance of others in order to feel good about yourself.

Social Circle

Friends and family are supposed to be good for you. They are there to share the good times with you and provide a support system when you are going through tough times. Various scientific studies show that people with strong friendships are less likely to suffer from stress and depression and generally have longer lifespans. However, your social circle is not always good for you. In some cases, your social circle might be the reason behind your negative attributes, including things like your anger problem.

There is a saying that you are the average of the closest five people you spend most of your time with. Therefore, if you have an anger problem, it might be time to look at your circle of friends and check whether they are fueling your anger problem when you are trying so hard to deal with it. There are a number of reasons why your circle of friends might exacerbate your anger problem.

First, your circle of friends influences your behavior. We often pick up behaviors from the people around us. If you spend most of your time around confident people, you might start becoming more confident, even if you were not very confident to begin with. Similarly, if you spend most of your time with people who tend to express their anger aggressively, you might start picking up this behavior from them. You might even have noticed that you tend to be more aggressive when you are with a certain group of friends.

Second, your group of friends can also infect you with negative emotions, including anger. Emotions are usually contagious. If you spend time with a happy person, you are more likely to start feeling happy. If you spend time with a grieving person, you will start feeling sad, even if you did not personally know the deceased. Similarly, if you spend most of your time with people who are generally angry, their emotional state will be transferred to you.

Finally, your circle of friends can also influence your beliefs. Even though our beliefs start forming from our childhood, they are constantly being reinforced or challenged. The more they are reinforced, the stronger they become, and the more they are challenged, the weaker they become. Beliefs that are constantly being challenged might even end up being abandoned altogether. Since your beliefs play a role in your ability to manage your anger, being around a social circle that reinforces your anger-inducing beliefs can exacerbate your anger problem.

Chapter Summary

- There are some other factors that might worsen your anger problem. Being aware of these factors can keep you from sabotaging your efforts of managing your anger problem.

- Alcohol fuels your anger problem by reducing your ability to correctly judge the intentions of other, making you more aggressive, reducing your ability to consider the long-term consequences of your actions and making your anger more tolerable.

- Drug abuse also fuels an anger problem. Drugs provide an escape and lead to unhealthy ways of anger expression.

- Drug abuse can also fuel an anger problem through family conflicts, guilt, withdrawal, or through their effect on the brain.

- Negative thoughts distort your view of the world and increase your chances of getting angry.

- Your beliefs determine your behavior, and can sometimes increase your inclination to respond to situations with anger.

- Your social circle might also fuel your anger by influencing your behavior, infecting you with negative emotions and influencing your beliefs.

Final Words

Thank you for sticking with me to the end of this book.

By now, I believe you are well-equipped with all the knowledge and information you need to deal with your anger problem. You know what anger is and the different types of anger, you know where anger comes from, you can recognize the signs and symptoms of an anger problem, you know why anger is not good for you and you know the common myths and misconceptions that people hold about anger. In addition, you have learned how to stop being easily irritable, how to get to the root cause of your anger, and how to let off your anger without hurting others. You have also learned 9 secrets from ancient Buddhist monks on how to deal with your anger, how to resolve conflicts within the family, how to let go of grudges and the factors that may fuel your anger problem.

However, any knowledge is only as good as what you choose to do with it. If you gain knowledge but then decide to sit on it, you won't see any change in your life. On the other hand, if you choose to act on it, you have the power to change your life. I now want you to take the knowledge that you have learned in this book and start applying it in your life, and I can guarantee you that you are going to see a dramatic change in your life for the better.

Lastly, I would greatly appreciate it if you could leave your honest feedback for this book on Amazon. It will only take you a few minutes and will help me keep producing such great books for you.

Cheers to controlling your anger, taming your inner lion and healthier, happier relationships!

Made in the USA
San Bernardino,
CA